Piano & Keyboard Chords

Easy-to-Use, Easy-to-Carry
One Chord on EVERY page

Edited by Jake Jackson

FLAME TREE
PUBLISHING

Produced and created by
FLAME TREE PUBLISHING
Crabtree Hall, Crabtree Lane
Fulham, London, SW6 6TY
United Kingdom
www.flametreepublishing.com

See our music information site:
www.musicfirebox.com

First Published in 2007

Publisher & Creative Director: Nick Wells
Editor: Polly Willis
Designer: Jake

10 09

9 10 8

Flame Tree Publishing is part of the
Foundry Creative Media Company Limited

ISBN 978-1-84451-715-2

Printed in China

Contents

As a keyboard player, even if you only ever play single-note solos, it is essential that you know your chords – they are the building blocks behind all musical compositions. All melodies have their roots in chords and chordal progressions.

The main part of the book provides one chord per page for easy reference, and includes hundreds of chords suitable for many different styles of music.

Name and abbreviation of the chord.

Use the tabs on the side/bottom of each page to find the chord you want quickly.

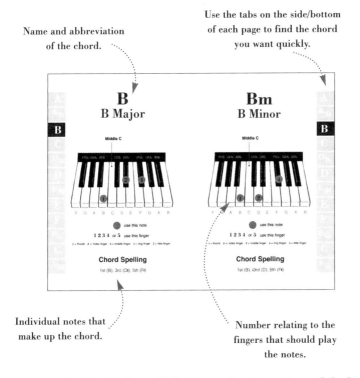

Individual notes that make up the chord.

Number relating to the fingers that should play the notes.

At the end of the book you'll find some first inversions of the basic major and minor triads.

How To Use The Keyboard Diagrams

The keyboard diagrams in this book will help you to learn the shapes of hundreds of chords, and will be a useful reference guide when you are playing and composing your own music. This is by no means a comprehensive manual, but should provide enough chord formations to keep even the most advanced musician busy!

While it might seem dull learning the fingerings, remember that the wider your chord vocabulary becomes, the more you will be able to vary your playing style and compositions. As well as providing you with a wide variety of chords to use whether you are into pop, rock, jazz or blues, it is particularly important to know your chords if you are planning to play with other musicians – you don't want to be left struggling to find the right chord while the other musicians are halfway through the next verse.

The chords are divided by key, from C to B. The name and abbreviation of the chord is shown at the top of the page, and notes that are included in the chord are shown below the keyboard.

The red circles on the diagram indicate which finger to use to play the notes in the right hand. The blue circles below the chord spelling indicate which finger to use to play the notes in the left hand. This is explained further on the opposite page.

Which Finger Shall I Use?

The diagrams in the book suggest which finger to use to play each note. The notes to be played in the right hand will be shown in red circles on the keyboard diagram.

Most of the chords use only the right hand, but some of the more advanced chords (9th, 11th and 13th chords) use both hands. When two hands are required, the red circles on the diagram will indicate what to play in the right hand and blue circles below the chord spelling will indicate what to play in the left hand.

The fingering is the same for the right and the left hand:

1 = thumb   2 = index finger   3 = middle finger   4 = ring finger   5 = little finger

On the keyboard it will look like this:

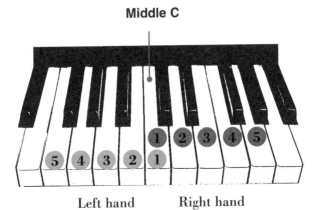

Left hand   Right hand

The Note Names

Although we will include the names of the notes above/below each keyboard diagram, we thought it would be useful to include layouts of the keyboard which show the names of the notes. We will show the sharps and flats (or black notes) on separate diagrams.

The White Notes (naturals)

The Black Notes (sharps/♯)

The Black Notes (flats/♭)

The Left Hand

In most of the examples we have given in this book, the right hand is used to play each chord. To provide an accompaniment to each chord, we suggest that the left hand plays the bottom (bass) note of each chord. In addition to this, you could add a further note, as in the example below. This is the 8th note above the given bass note. To create a fuller, richer sound, you could also include a note that you are playing in the right hand with the two notes you are playing in the left hand. As you become more confident and familiar with the harmonies, you could experiment by adding further notes into the mix.

This example shows the left-hand accompaniment that could be played with the C chords you will find in the book.

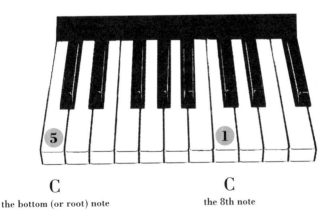

C
the bottom (or root) note

C
the 8th note

For a small number of the more advanced chords we have included (9th, 11th and 13th chords) this left-hand accompaniment will not be suitable as you will require two hands to play them.

C
C Major

Middle C

C D E F G A B C D E F

use this note

1 2 3 4 or **5** use this finger

1 = thumb   2 = index finger   3 = middle finger   4 = ring finger   5 = little finger

Chord Spelling

1st (C), 3rd (E), 5th (G)

Cm
C Minor

Middle C

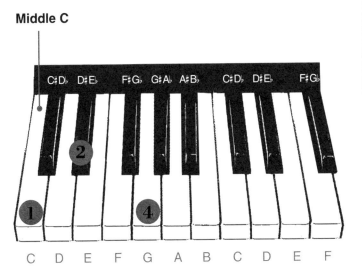

use this note

1 2 3 4 or **5** use this finger

1 = thumb 2 = index finger 3 = middle finger 4 = ring finger 5 = little finger

Chord Spelling

1st (C), ♭3rd (E♭), 5th (G)

C+/Caug
C Augmented Triad

A
B♭/A♯
B
C
C♯/D♭
D
E♭/D♯
E
F
F♯/G♭
G
A♭/G♯

Middle C

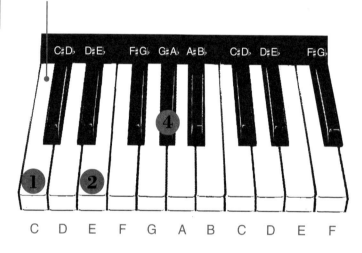

use this note

1 2 3 4 or **5** use this finger

1 = thumb   2 = index finger   3 = middle finger   4 = ring finger   5 = little finger

Chord Spelling

1st (C), 3rd (E), ♯5th (G♯)

Csus4
C Suspended 4th

Middle C

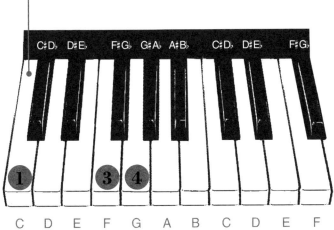

use this note

1 2 3 4 or **5** use this finger

1 = thumb   2 = index finger   3 = middle finger   4 = ring finger   5 = little finger

Chord Spelling

1st (C), 4th (F), 5th (G)

A

B♭/A♯

B

C

C♯/D♭

D

E♭/D♯

E

F

F♯/G♭

G

A♭/G♯

Co/Cdim
C Diminished Triad

Middle C

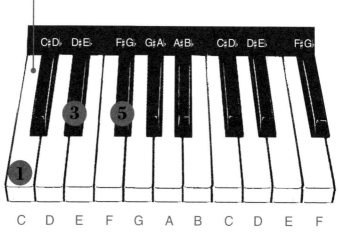

C D E F G A B C D E F

use this note

1 2 3 4 or **5** use this finger

1 = thumb   2 = index finger   3 = middle finger   4 = ring finger   5 = little finger

Chord Spelling

1st (C), ♭3rd (E♭), ♭5th (G♭)

C6
C Major 6th

A
B♭/A♯
B
C
C♯/D♭
D
E♭/D♯
E
F
F♯/G♭
G
A♭/G♯

Middle C

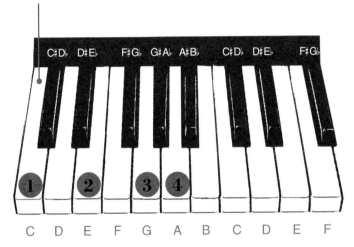

C D E F G A B C D E F

use this note

1 2 3 4 or **5**   use this finger

1 = thumb   2 = index finger   3 = middle finger   4 = ring finger   5 = little finger

Chord Spelling

1st (C), 3rd (E), 5th (G), 6th (A)

Cm6
C Minor 6th

Middle C

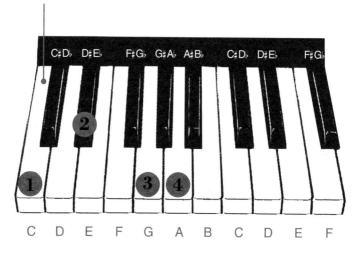

C D E F G A B C D E F

 use this note

1 2 3 4 or **5** use this finger

1 = thumb 2 = index finger 3 = middle finger 4 = ring finger 5 = little finger

Chord Spelling

1st (C), ♭3rd (E♭), 5th (G), 6th (A)

Cmaj7
C Major 7th

Middle C

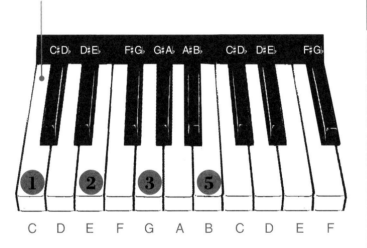

use this note

1 2 3 4 or **5** use this finger

1 = thumb 2 = index finger 3 = middle finger 4 = ring finger 5 = little finger

Chord Spelling

1st (C), 3rd (E), 5th (G), 7th (B)

Cm7
C Minor 7th

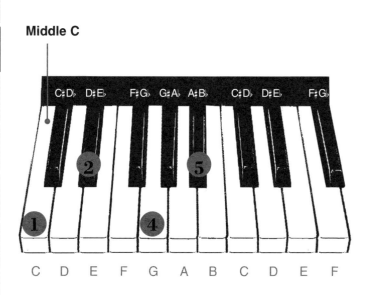

Middle C

C♯D♭ D♯E♭ F♯G♭ G♯A♭ A♯B♭ C♯D♭ D♯E♭ F♯G♭

2   5

1   4

C D E F G A B C D E F

● use this note

1 2 3 4 or **5** use this finger

1 = thumb 2 = index finger 3 = middle finger 4 = ring finger 5 = little finger

Chord Spelling

1st (C), ♭3rd (E♭), 5th (G), ♭7th (B♭)

A
B♭/A♯
B
C
C♯/D♭
D
E♭/D♯
E
F
F♯/G♭
G
A♭/G♯

C7
C Dominant 7th

Middle C

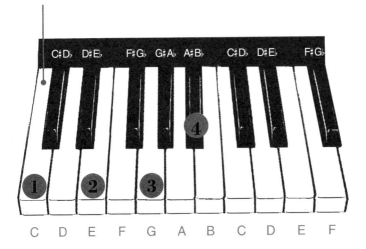

use this note

1 2 3 4 or **5** use this finger

1 = thumb   2 = index finger   3 = middle finger   4 = ring finger   5 = little finger

Chord Spelling

1st (C), 3rd (E), 5th (G), ♭7th (B♭)

C7sus4

C Dominant 7th sus4

Middle C

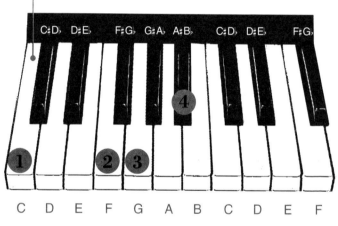

use this note

1 2 3 4 or **5** use this finger

1 = thumb   2 = index finger   3 = middle finger   4 = ring finger   5 = little finger

Chord Spelling

1st (C), 4th (F), 5th (G), ♭7th (B♭)

C7+5
C Dominant 7th
Augmented 5th

Middle C

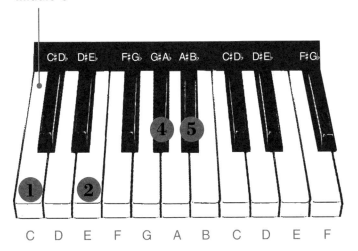

 use this note

1 2 3 4 or **5** use this finger

1 = thumb 2 = index finger 3 = middle finger 4 = ring finger 5 = little finger

Chord Spelling

1st (C), 3rd (E), #5th (G#), ♭7th (B♭)

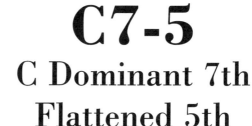

C7-5
C Dominant 7th
Flattened 5th

Middle C

| C♯D♭ | D♯E♭ | | F♯G♭ | G♯A♭ | A♯B♭ | | C♯D♭ | D♯E♭ | | F♯G♭ |

4   **5**

1   **2**

C   D   E   F   G   A   B   C   D   E   F

use this note

1 2 3 4 or **5**   use this finger

1 = thumb   2 = index finger   3 = middle finger   4 = ring finger   5 = little finger

Chord Spelling

1st (C), 3rd (E), ♭5th (G♭), ♭7th (B♭)

A
B♭/A♯
B
C
C♯/D♭
D
E♭/D♯
E
F
F♯/G♭
G
A♭/G♯

Cdim7
C Diminished 7th

A
B♭/A#
B
C
C#/D♭
D
E♭/D#
E
F
F#/G♭
G
A♭/G#

Middle C

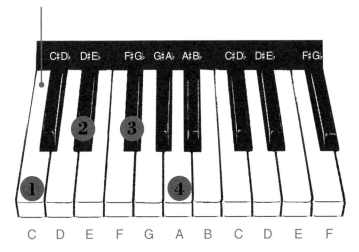

C#D♭ D#E♭   F#G♭ G#A♭ A#B♭   C#D♭ D#E♭   F#G♭

C D E F G A B C D E F

use this note

1 2 3 4 or **5** use this finger

1 = thumb 2 = index finger 3 = middle finger 4 = ring finger 5 = little finger

Chord Spelling

1st (C), ♭3rd (E♭), ♭5th (G♭), ♭♭7th (B♭♭)

Cm7-5
C Minor 7th
Flattened 5th

Middle C

| C♯D♭ | D♯E♭ | | F♯G♭ | G♯A♭ | A♯B♭ | | C♯D♭ | D♯E♭ | | F♯G♭ |

C D E F G A B C D E F

use this note

1 2 3 4 or **5** use this finger

1 = thumb   2 = index finger   3 = middle finger   4 = ring finger   5 = little finger

Chord Spelling

1st (C), ♭3rd (E♭), ♭5th (G♭), ♭7th (B♭)

Cmmaj7
C Minor-Major 7th

Middle C

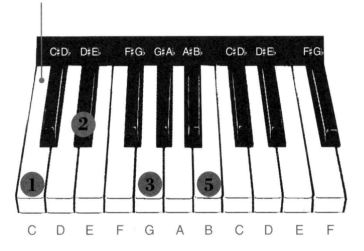

C D E F G A B C D E F

🔘 use this note

1 2 3 4 or **5** use this finger

1 = thumb 2 = index finger 3 = middle finger 4 = ring finger 5 = little finger

Chord Spelling

1st (C), ♭3rd (E♭), 5th (G), 7th (B)

Cmaj9
C Major 9th

Middle C

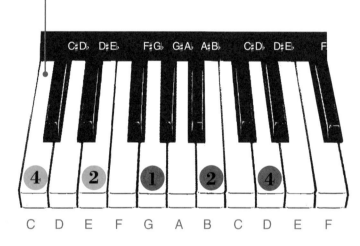

C D E F G A B C D E F

 use this note

1 2 3 4 or **5** use this finger

1 = thumb **2** = index finger **3** = middle finger **4** = ring finger **5** = little finger

Chord Spelling

1st (C), 3rd (E), 5th (G), 7th (B), 9th (D)

Cm9
C Minor 9th

A

B♭/A#

B

C

C#/D♭

D

E♭/D#

E

F

F#/G♭

G

A♭/G#

Middle C

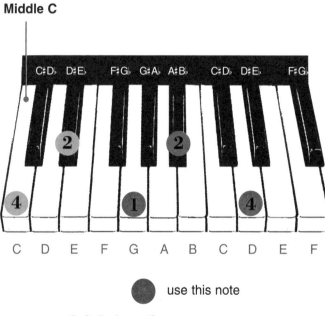

use this note

1 2 3 4 or **5** use this finger

1 = thumb   2 = index finger   3 = middle finger   4 = ring finger   5 = little finger

Chord Spelling

1st (C), ♭3rd (E♭), 5th (G), ♭7th (B♭), 9th (D)

C9
C Dominant 9th

Middle C

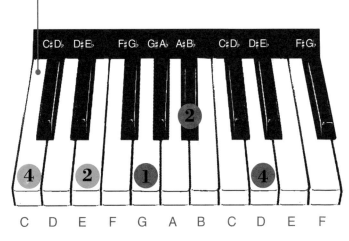

C♯D♭ D♯E♭ F♯G♭ G♯A♭ A♯B♭ C♯D♭ D♯E♭ F♯G♭

C D E F G A B C D E F

use this note

1 2 3 4 or **5** use this finger

1 = thumb 2 = index finger 3 = middle finger 4 = ring finger 5 = little finger

Chord Spelling

1st (C), 3rd (E), 5th (G), ♭7th (B♭), 9th (D)

C9+5
C 9th Augmented 5th

Middle C

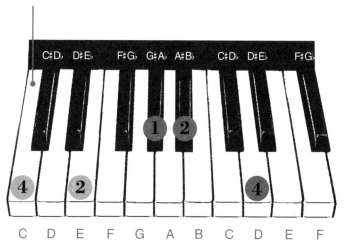

use this note

1 2 3 4 or **5** use this finger

1 = thumb 2 = index finger 3 = middle finger 4 = ring finger 5 = little finger

Chord Spelling

1st (C), 3rd (E), #5th (G#), ♭7th (B♭), 9th (D)

C9-5
C 9th Flattened 5th

Middle C

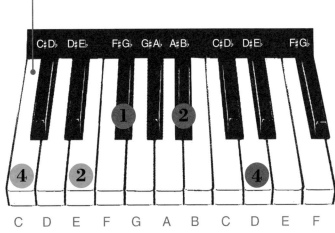

C D E F G A B C D E F

● use this note

1 2 3 4 or **5** use this finger

1 = thumb   2 = index finger   3 = middle finger   4 = ring finger   5 = little finger

Chord Spelling

1st (C), 3rd (E), ♭5th (G♭), ♭7th (B♭), 9th (D)

C9/6
C 9th Add 6th

Middle C

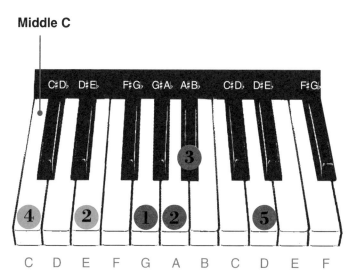

C D E F G A B C D E F

use this note

1 2 3 4 or **5** use this finger

1 = thumb   2 = index finger   3 = middle finger   4 = ring finger   5 = little finger

Chord Spelling

1st (C), 3rd (E), 5th (G), 6th (A), ♭7th (B♭), 9th (D)

Cmaj11
C Major 11th

Middle C

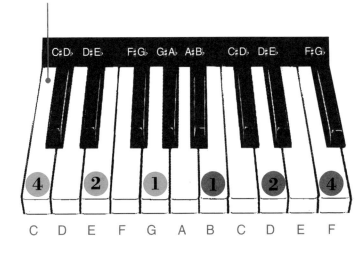

use this note

1 2 3 4 or **5** use this finger

1 = thumb   2 = index finger   3 = middle finger   4 = ring finger   5 = little finger

Chord Spelling

1st (C), 3rd (E), 5th (G), 7th (B), 9th (D), 11th (F)

Cm11
C Minor 11th

A
B♭/A♯
B
C
C♯/D♭
D
E♭/D♯
E
F
F♯/G♭
G
A♭/G♯

Middle C

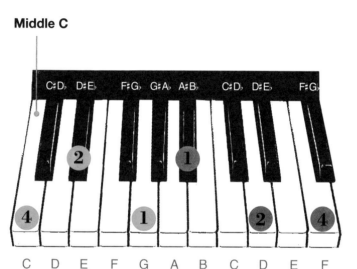

use this note

1 2 3 4 or **5** use this finger

1 = thumb 2 = index finger 3 = middle finger 4 = ring finger 5 = little finger

Chord Spelling

1st (C), ♭3rd (E♭), 5th (G), ♭7th (B♭), 9th (D), 11th (F)

C11
C Dominant 11th

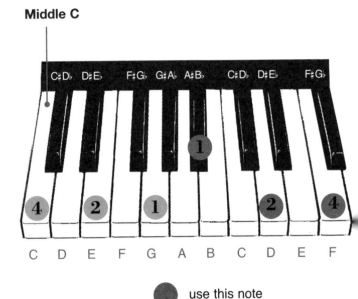

Middle C

C♯D♭ D♯E♭   F♯G♭ G♯A♭ A♯B♭   C♯D♭ D♯E♭   F♯G♭

C D E F G A B C D E F

use this note

1 2 3 4 or **5** use this finger

1 = thumb   2 = index finger   3 = middle finger   4 = ring finger   5 = little finger

Chord Spelling

1st (C), 3rd (E), 5th (G), ♭7th (B♭), 9th (D), 11th (F)

C11-9
C 11th Flattened 9th

A
B♭/A♯
B
C
C♯/D♭
D
E♭/D♯
E
F
E♯/G♭
G
G♯/A♭

Middle C

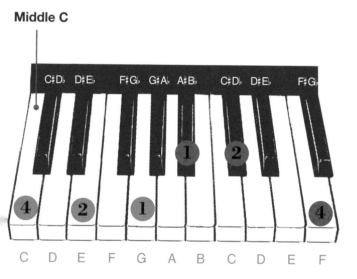

use this note

1 2 3 4 or **5** use this finger

1 = thumb   2 = index finger   3 = middle finger   4 = ring finger   5 = little finger

Chord Spelling

1st (C), 3rd (E), 5th (G), ♭7th (B♭), ♭9th (D♭), 11th (F)

Cmaj13
C Major 13th

Middle C

F♯G♭ G♯A♭ A♯B♭　C♯D♭ D♯E♭　F♯G♭ G♯A♭ A♯B♭

F G A B C D E F G A B

⬤ use this note

1 2 3 4 or **5** use this finger

1 = thumb　2 = index finger　3 = middle finger　4 = ring finger　5 = little finger

Chord Spelling

1st (C), 3rd (E), 5th (G), 7th (B), 9th (D), 11th (F), 13th (A)

Cm13
C Minor 13th

Middle C

F G A B C D E F G A B

⬤ use this note

1 2 3 4 or **5** use this finger

1 = thumb 2 = index finger 3 = middle finger 4 = ring finger 5 = little finger

Chord Spelling

1st (C), ♭3rd (E♭), 5th (G), ♭7th (B♭), 9th (D), 11th (F), 13th (A)

C13
C Dominant 13th

Middle C

F#G♭ G#A♭ A#B♭　　C#D♭ D#E♭　　F#G♭ G#A♭ A#B♭

F G A B C D E F G A B

1　**2**　**3**　**5**

○ use this note

1 2 3 4 or **5**　use this finger

1 = thumb　2 = index finger　3 = middle finger　4 = ring finger　5 = little finger

Chord Spelling

1st (C), 3rd (E), 5th (G), ♭7th (B♭), 9th (D), 11th (F), 13th (

C13-9
C 13th Flattened 9th

Middle C

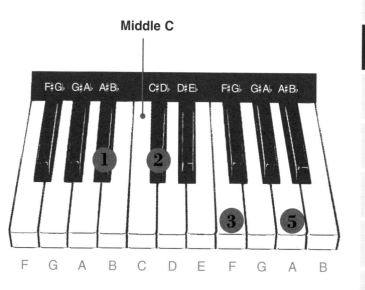

use this note

1 2 3 4 or **5** use this finger

1 = thumb 2 = index finger 3 = middle finger 4 = ring finger 5 = little finger

Chord Spelling

(C), 3rd (E), 5th (G), ♭7th (B♭), ♭9th (D♭), 11th (F), 13th (A)

C#
C# Major

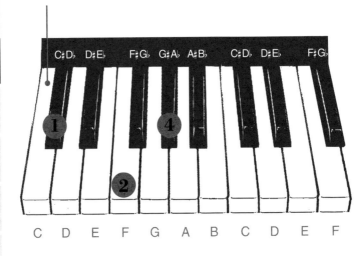

Middle C

C#D♭ D#E♭   F#G♭ G#A♭ A#B♭   C#D♭ D#E♭   F#G♭

C D E F G A B C D E F

⬤ use this note

1 2 3 4 or **5** use this finger

1 = thumb 2 = index finger 3 = middle finger 4 = ring finger 5 = little finger

Chord Spelling

1st (C#), 3rd (E#), 5th (G#)

C#m
C# Minor

Middle C

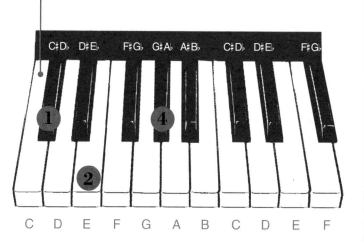

C   D   E   F   G   A   B   C   D   E   F

● use this note

1 2 3 4 or **5** use this finger

1 = thumb   2 = index finger   3 = middle finger   4 = ring finger   5 = little finger

Chord Spelling

1st (C#), ♭3rd (E), 5th (G#)

C♯+/C♯aug
C♯ Augmented Triad

Middle C

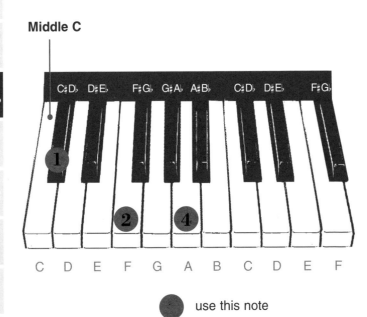

C D E F G A B C D E F

🔴 use this note

1 2 3 4 or **5** use this finger

1 = thumb 2 = index finger 3 = middle finger 4 = ring finger 5 = little finger

Chord Spelling

1st (C♯), 3rd (E♯), ♯5th (Gx)

C#sus4
C# Suspended 4th

Middle C

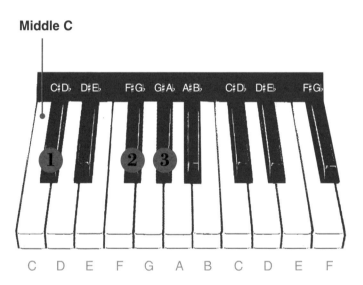

C D E F G A B C D E F

use this note

1 2 3 4 or **5** use this finger

1 = thumb   2 = index finger   3 = middle finger   4 = ring finger   5 = little finger

Chord Spelling

1st (C#), 4th (F#), 5th (G#)

C#o/C#dim
C# Diminished Triad

Middle C

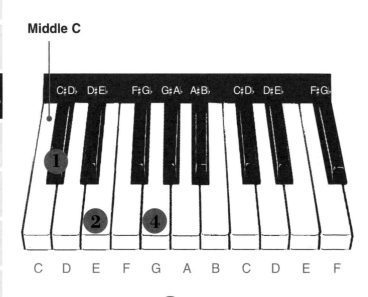

C D E F G A B C D E F

● use this note

1 2 3 4 or **5** use this finger

1 = thumb 2 = index finger 3 = middle finger 4 = ring finger 5 = little finger

Chord Spelling

1st (C#), b3rd (E), b5th (G)

C#6
C# Major 6th

Middle C

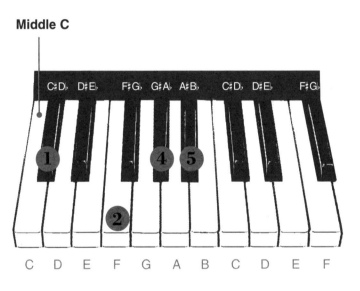

use this note

1 2 3 4 or **5** use this finger

1 = thumb 2 = index finger 3 = middle finger 4 = ring finger 5 = little finger

Chord Spelling

1st (C#), 3rd (E#), 5th (G#), 6th (A#)

C#m6
C# Minor 6th

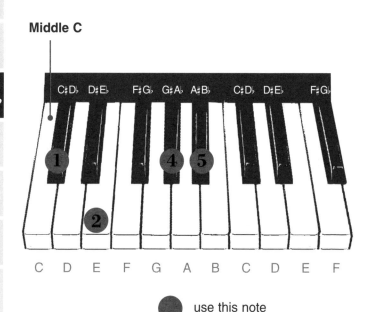

Middle C

C#D♭ D#E♭   F#G♭ G#A♭ A#B♭   C#D♭ D#E♭   F#G♭

C D E F G A B C D E F

use this note

1 2 3 4 or 5 use this finger

1 = thumb 2 = index finger 3 = middle finger 4 = ring finger 5 = little finger

Chord Spelling

1st (C#), ♭3rd (E), 5th (G#), 6th (A#)

C#maj7
C# Major 7th

Middle C

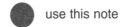

C#D♭ D#E♭   F#G♭ G#A♭ A#B♭   C#D♭ D#E♭   F#G♭

C   D   E   F   G   A   B   C   D   E   F

use this note

1 2 3 4 or **5** use this finger

1 = thumb 2 = index finger 3 = middle finger 4 = ring finger 5 = little finger

Chord Spelling

1st (C#), 3rd (E#), 5th (G#), 7th (B#)

A
B♭/A#
B
C
C#/D♭
D
E♭/D#
E
F
F#/G♭
G

C♯m7
C♯ Minor 7th

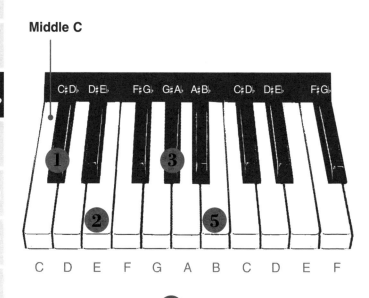

Middle C

C D E F G A B C D E F

⬤ use this note

1 2 3 4 or **5** use this finger

1 = thumb 2 = index finger 3 = middle finger 4 = ring finger 5 = little finger

Chord Spelling

1st (C♯), ♭3rd (E), 5th (G♯), ♭7th (B)

C#7
C# Dominant 7th

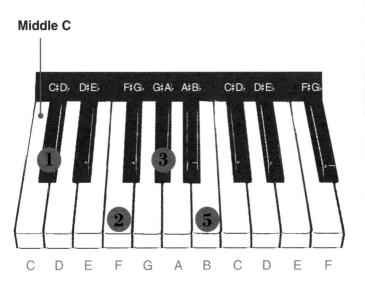

Middle C

use this note

1 2 3 4 or **5**   use this finger

1 = thumb   2 = index finger   3 = middle finger   4 = ring finger   5 = little finger

Chord Spelling

1st (C#), 3rd (E#), 5th (G#), ♭7th (B)

C#7sus4
C# Dominant 7th sus4

Middle C

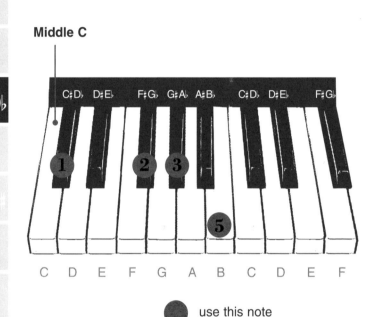

C D E F G A B C D E F

🔴 use this note

1 2 3 4 or **5** use this finger

1 = thumb   2 = index finger   3 = middle finger   4 = ring finger   5 = little finger

Chord Spelling

1st (C#), 4th (F#), 5th (G#), ♭7th (B)

C♯7+5
C♯ Dominant 7th
Augmented 5th

Middle C

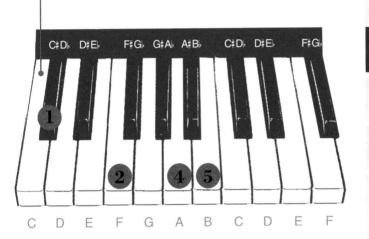

use this note

1 2 3 4 or **5** use this finger

1 = thumb   2 = index finger   3 = middle finger   4 = ring finger   5 = little finger

Chord Spelling

1st (C♯), 3rd (E♯), ♯5th (Gx), ♭7th (B)

C#7-5
C# Dominant 7th
Flattened 5th

Middle C

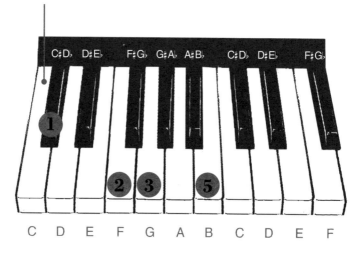

use this note

1 2 3 4 or **5** use this finger

1 = thumb   2 = index finger   3 = middle finger   4 = ring finger   5 = little finger

Chord Spelling

1st (C#), 3rd (E#), ♭5th (G), ♭7th (B)

C#dim7
C# Diminished 7th

Middle C

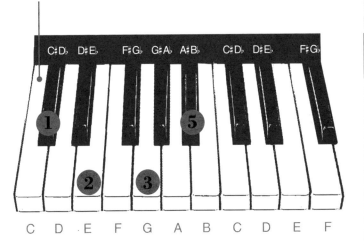

C D E F G A B C D E F

use this note

1 2 3 4 or **5**   use this finger

1 = thumb   2 = index finger   3 = middle finger   4 = ring finger   5 = little finger

Chord Spelling

1st (C#), ♭3rd (E), ♭5th (G), ♭♭7th (B♭)

C♯m7-5
C♯ Minor 7th
Flattened 5th

Middle C

use this note

1 2 3 4 or **5** use this finger

1 = thumb   2 = index finger   3 = middle finger   4 = ring finger   5 = little finger

Chord Spelling

1st (C♯), ♭3rd (E), ♭5th (G), ♭7th (B)

C#mmaj7
C# Minor-Major 7th

Middle C

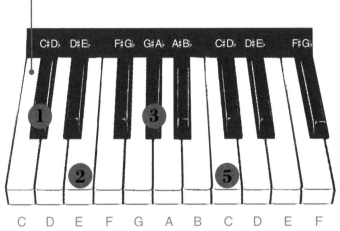

C D E F G A B C D E F

use this note

1 2 3 4 or **5** use this finger

1 = thumb 2 = index finger 3 = middle finger 4 = ring finger 5 = little finger

Chord Spelling

1st (C#), ♭3rd (E), 5th (G#), 7th (B#)

C#maj9
C# Major 9th

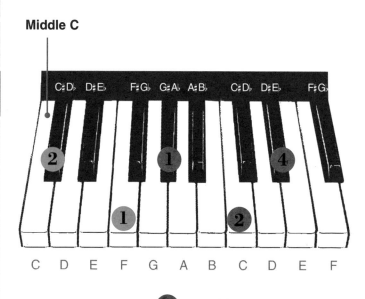

Middle C

use this note

1 2 3 4 or **5** use this finger

1 = thumb 2 = index finger 3 = middle finger 4 = ring finger 5 = little finger

Chord Spelling

1st (C#), 3rd (E#), 5th (G#), 7th (B#), 9th (D#)

C#m9
C# Minor 9th

Middle C

C D E F G A B C D E F

● use this note

1 2 3 4 or **5** use this finger

1 = thumb 2 = index finger 3 = middle finger 4 = ring finger 5 = little finger

Chord Spelling

1st (C#), b3rd (E), 5th (G#), b7th (B), 9th (D#)

A
Bb/A#
B
C
C#/Db
D
Eb/D#
E
F
F#/Gb
G
Ab/G#

C#9

C# Dominant 9th

Middle C

C#D♭ D#E♭   F#G♭ G#A♭ A#B♭   C#D♭ D#E♭   F#G♭

2   **1**   **4**

1   **2**

C D E F G A B C D E F

● use this note

1 2 3 4 or **5** use this finger

1 = thumb   2 = index finger   3 = middle finger   4 = ring finger   5 = little finger

Chord Spelling

1st (C#), 3rd (E#), 5th (G#), ♭7th (B), 9th (D#)

C#9+5
C# 9th Augmented 5th

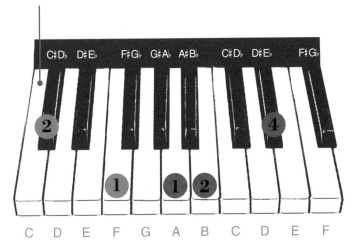

Middle C

use this note

1 2 3 4 or **5** use this finger

1 = thumb **2** = index finger **3** = middle finger **4** = ring finger **5** = little finger

Chord Spelling

1st (C#), 3rd (E#), #5th (Gx), b7th (B), 9th (D#)

C#9-5
C# 9th Flattened 5th

Middle C

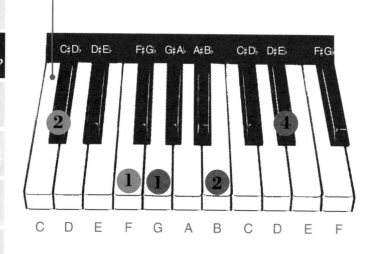

C D E F G A B C D E F

● use this note

1 2 3 4 or **5** use this finger

1 = thumb 2 = index finger 3 = middle finger 4 = ring finger 5 = little finger

Chord Spelling

1st (C#), 3rd (E#), ♭5th (G), ♭7th (B), 9th (D#)

C♯9/6
C♯ 9th Add 6th

Middle C

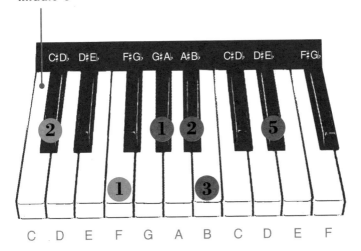

use this note

1 2 3 4 or **5** use this finger

1 = thumb   2 = index finger   3 = middle finger   4 = ring finger   5 = little finger

Chord Spelling

1st (C♯), 3rd (E♯), 5th (G♯), 6th (A♯), ♭7th (B), 9th (D♯)

C♯maj11
C♯ Major 11th

Middle C

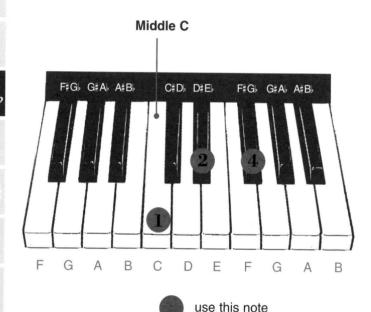

F G A B C D E F G A B

● use this note

1 2 3 4 or **5** use this finger

1 = thumb   2 = index finger   3 = middle finger   4 = ring finger   5 = little finger

Chord Spelling

1st (C♯), 3rd (E♯), 5th (G♯), 7th (B♯), 9th (D♯), 11th (F♯)

C♯m11
C♯ Minor 11th

Middle C

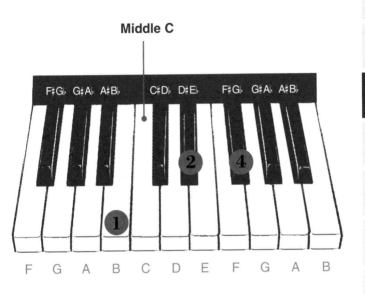

use this note

1 2 3 4 or **5** use this finger

1 = thumb 2 = index finger 3 = middle finger 4 = ring finger 5 = little finger

Chord Spelling

1st (C♯), ♭3rd (E), 5th (G♯), ♭7th (B), 9th (D♯), 11th (F♯)

C♯11
C♯ Dominant 11th

Middle C

use this note

1 2 3 4 or **5** use this finger

1 = thumb 2 = index finger 3 = middle finger 4 = ring finger 5 = little finger

Chord Spelling

1st (C♯), 3rd (E♯), 5th (G♯), ♭7th (B), 9th (D♯), 11th (F♯)

C#11-9
C# 11th Flattened 9th

Middle C

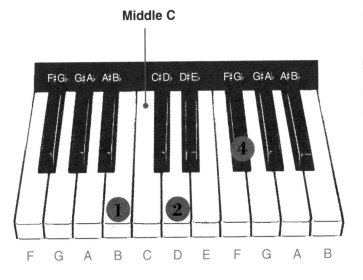

use this note

1 2 3 4 or **5** use this finger

1 = thumb   2 = index finger   3 = middle finger   4 = ring finger   5 = little finger

Chord Spelling

1st (C#), 3rd (E#), 5th (G#), ♭7th (B), ♭9th (D), 11th (F#)

C#maj13
C# Major 13th

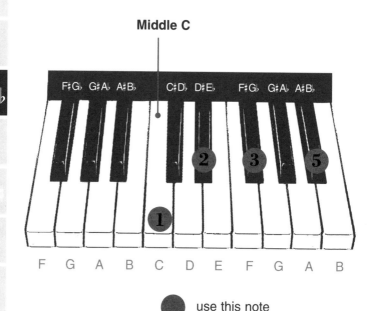

Middle C

use this note

1 2 3 4 or **5** use this finger

1 = thumb 2 = index finger 3 = middle finger 4 = ring finger 5 = little finger

Chord Spelling

1st (C#), 3rd (E#), 5th (G#), 7th (B#), 9th (D#), 11th (F#), 13th (A#)

C#m13
C# Minor 13th

Middle C

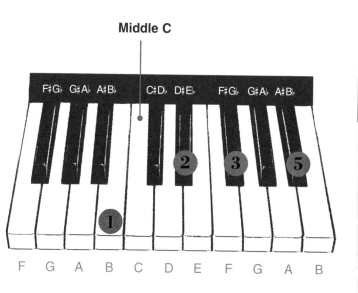

use this note

1 2 3 4 or **5** use this finger

1 = thumb 2 = index finger 3 = middle finger 4 = ring finger 5 = little finger

Chord Spelling

(C#), b3rd (E), 5th (G#), b7th (B), 9th (D#), 11th (F#), 13th (A#)

C#13
C# Dominant 13th

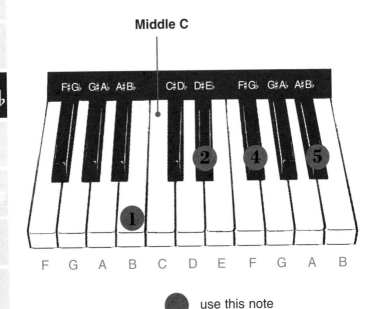

Middle C

use this note

1 2 3 4 or **5** use this finger

1 = thumb   2 = index finger   3 = middle finger   4 = ring finger   5 = little finger

Chord Spelling

1st (C#), 3rd (E#), 5th (G#), ♭7th (B), 9th (D#), 11th (F#), 13t

C#13-9
C# 13th Flattened 9th

Middle C

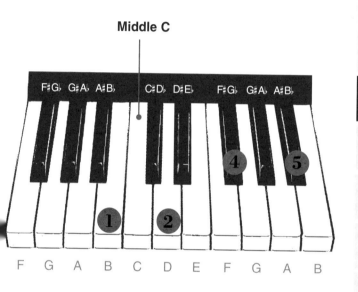

F G A B C D E F G A B

🔵 use this note

1 2 3 4 or **5** use this finger

1 = thumb 2 = index finger 3 = middle finger 4 = ring finger 5 = little finger

Chord Spelling

C#), 3rd (E#), 5th (G#), ♭7th (B), ♭9th (D), 11th (F#), 13th (A#)

D
D Major

Middle C

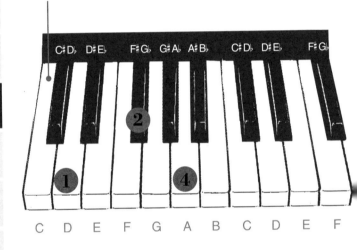

C D E F G A B C D E F

● use this note

1 2 3 4 or **5** use this finger

1 = thumb 2 = index finger 3 = middle finger 4 = ring finger 5 = little finger

Chord Spelling

1st (D), 3rd (F#), 5th (A)

Dm
D Minor

Middle C

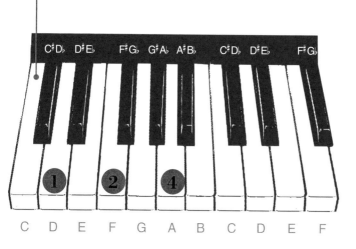

use this note

1 2 3 4 or **5** use this finger

1 = thumb   2 = index finger   3 = middle finger   4 = ring finger   5 = little finger

Chord Spelling

1st (D), ♭3rd (F), 5th (A)

D

D+/Daug
D Augmented Triad

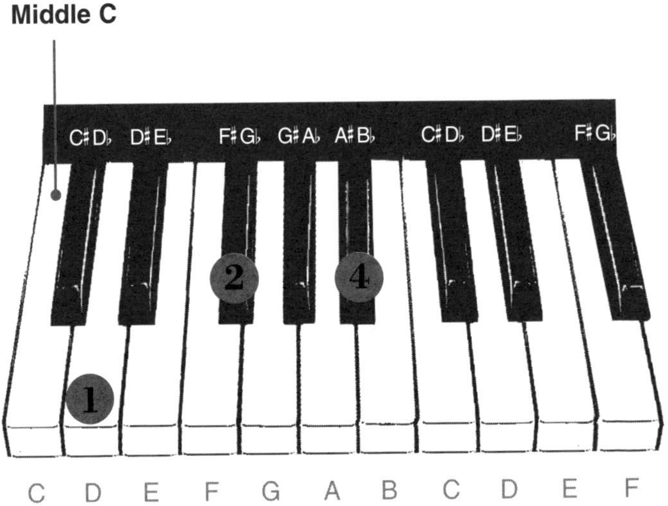

Middle C

use this note

1 2 3 4 or **5** use this finger

1 = thumb   2 = index finger   3 = middle finger   4 = ring finger   5 = little finger

Chord Spelling

1st (D), 3rd (F#), #5th (A#)

Dsus4
D Suspended 4th

Middle C

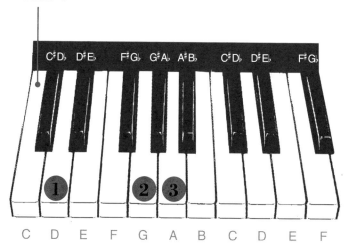

🔴 use this note

1 2 3 4 or **5** use this finger

1 = thumb   2 = index finger   3 = middle finger   4 = ring finger   5 = little finger

Chord Spelling

1st (D), 4th (G), 5th (A)

Do/Ddim
D Diminished Triad

Middle C

C D E F G A B C D E F

● use this note

1 2 3 4 or **5** use this finger

1 = thumb 2 = index finger 3 = middle finger 4 = ring finger 5 = little finger

Chord Spelling

1st (D), ♭3rd (F), ♭5th (A♭)

D6
D Major 6th

Middle C

C♯D♭ D♯E♭   F♯G♭ G♯A♭ A♯B♭   C♯D♭ D♯E♭   F♯G♭

C D E F G A B C D E F

use this note

1 2 3 4 or **5** use this finger

1 = thumb 2 = index finger 3 = middle finger 4 = ring finger 5 = little finger

Chord Spelling

1st (D), 3rd (F♯), 5th (A), 6th (B)

Dm6
D Minor 6th

Middle C

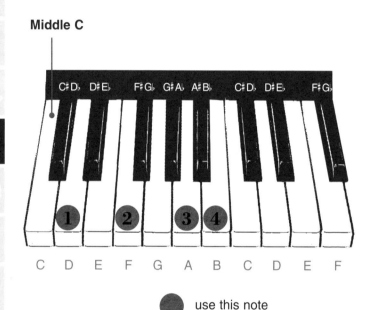

use this note

1 2 3 4 or **5** use this finger

1 = thumb 2 = index finger 3 = middle finger 4 = ring finger 5 = little finger

Chord Spelling

1st (D), ♭3rd (F), 5th (A), 6th (B)

Dmaj7
D Major 7th

Middle C

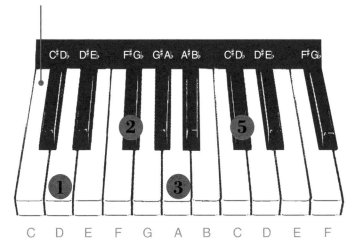

C D E F G A B C D E F

● use this note

1 2 3 4 or **5** use this finger

1 = thumb 2 = index finger 3 = middle finger 4 = ring finger 5 = little finger

Chord Spelling

1st (D), 3rd (F♯), 5th (A), 7th (C♯)

Dm7
D Minor 7th

Middle C

C♯D♭ D♯E♭   F♯G♭ G♯A♭ A♯B♭   C♯D♭ D♯E♭   F♯G♭

C D E F G A B C D E F

1 2 3 5

⬤ use this note

1 2 3 4 or **5** use this finger

1 = thumb   2 = index finger   3 = middle finger   4 = ring finger   5 = little finger

Chord Spelling

1st (D), ♭3rd (F), 5th (A), ♭7th (C)

D7
D Dominant 7th

Middle C

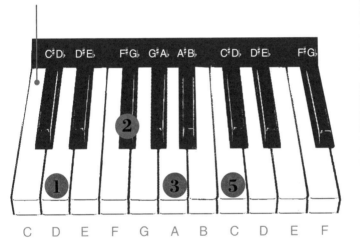

use this note

1 2 3 4 or **5** use this finger

1 = thumb   2 = index finger   3 = middle finger   4 = ring finger   5 = little finger

Chord Spelling

1st (D), 3rd (F♯), 5th (A), ♭7th (C)

D7sus4
D Dominant 7th sus4

Middle C

C D E F G A B C D E F

● use this note

1 2 3 4 or **5** use this finger

1 = thumb 2 = index finger 3 = middle finger 4 = ring finger 5 = little finger

Chord Spelling

1st (D), 4th (G), 5th (A), ♭7th (C)

D7+5
D Dominant 7th
Augmented 5th

Middle C

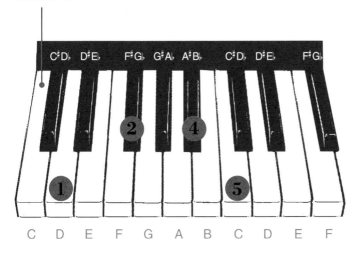

use this note

1 2 3 4 or **5** use this finger

1 = thumb 2 = index finger 3 = middle finger 4 = ring finger 5 = little finger

Chord Spelling

1st (D), 3rd (F#), #5th (A#), ♭7th (C)

D7-5
D Dominant 7th
Flattened 5th

Middle C

use this note

1 2 3 4 or **5** use this finger

1 = thumb 2 = index finger 3 = middle finger 4 = ring finger 5 = little finger

Chord Spelling

1st (D), 3rd (F#), ♭5th (A♭), ♭7th (C)

Ddim7
D Diminished 7th

Middle C

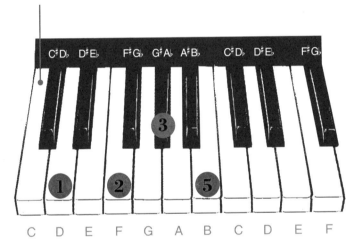

use this note

1 2 3 4 or **5** use this finger

1 = thumb   2 = index finger   3 = middle finger   4 = ring finger   5 = little finger

Chord Spelling

1st (D), b3rd (F), b5th (Ab), bb7th (B)

Dm7-5
D Minor 7th
Flattened 5th

Middle C

C D E F G A B C D E F

use this note

1 2 3 4 or 5 use this finger

1 = thumb 2 = index finger 3 = middle finger 4 = ring finger 5 = little finger

Chord Spelling

1st (D), ♭3rd (F), ♭5th (A♭), ♭7th (C)

Dmmaj7
D Minor-Major 7th

Middle C

C D E F G A B C D E F

use this note

1 2 3 4 or **5** use this finger

1 = thumb 2 = index finger 3 = middle finger 4 = ring finger 5 = little finger

Chord Spelling

1st (D), ♭3rd (F), 5th (A), 7th (C♯)

Dmaj9
D Major 9th

Middle C

use this note

1 2 3 4 or **5** use this finger

1 = thumb   2 = index finger   3 = middle finger   4 = ring finger   5 = little finger

Chord Spelling

1st (D), 3rd (F♯), 5th (A), 7th (C♯), 9th (E)

Dm9
D Minor 9th

Middle C

use this note

1 2 3 4 or **5** use this finger

1 = thumb   2 = index finger   3 = middle finger   4 = ring finger   5 = little finger

Chord Spelling

1st (D), ♭3rd (F), 5th (A), ♭7th (C), 9th (E)

D9
D Dominant 9th

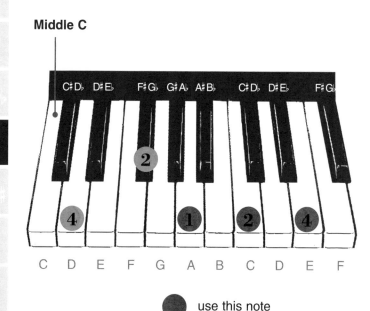

Middle C

C♯D♭ D♯E♭ F♯G♭ G♯A♭ A♯B♭ C♯D♭ D♯E♭ F♯G♭

C D E F G A B C D E F

use this note

1 2 3 4 or **5** use this finger

1 = thumb **2** = index finger **3** = middle finger **4** = ring finger **5** = little finger

Chord Spelling

1st (D), 3rd (F♯), 5th (A), ♭7th (C), 9th (E)

D9+5
D 9th Augmented 5th

Middle C

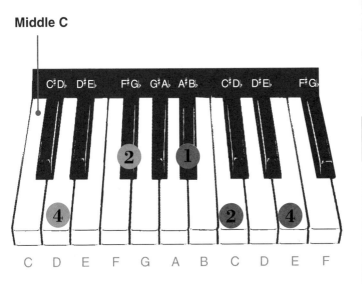

use this note

1 2 3 4 or **5**   use this finger

1 = thumb   2 = index finger   3 = middle finger   4 = ring finger   5 = little finger

Chord Spelling

1st (D), 3rd (F#), #5th (A#), ♭7th (C), 9th (E)

D9-5
D 9th Flattened 5th

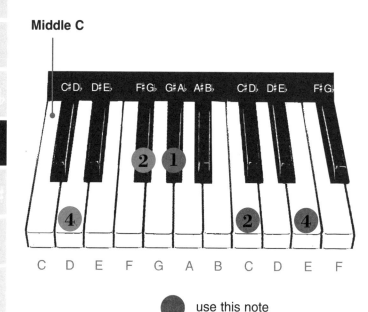

Middle C

use this note

1 2 3 4 or **5** use this finger

1 = thumb 2 = index finger 3 = middle finger 4 = ring finger 5 = little finger

Chord Spelling

1st (D), 3rd (F#), ♭5th (A♭), ♭7th (C), 9th (E)

D9/6
D 9th Add 6th

Middle C

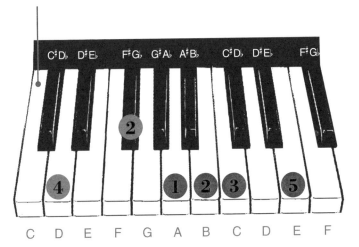

C D E F G A B C D E F

● use this note

1 2 3 4 or **5** use this finger

1 = thumb 2 = index finger 3 = middle finger 4 = ring finger 5 = little finger

Chord Spelling

1st (D), 3rd (F♯), 5th (A), 6th (B), ♭7th (C), 9th (E)

Dmaj11
D Major 11th

Middle C

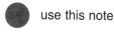

F G A B C D E F G A B

use this note

1 2 3 4 or **5** use this finger

1 = thumb 2 = index finger 3 = middle finger 4 = ring finger 5 = little finger

Chord Spelling

1st (D), 3rd (F♯), 5th (A), 7th (C♯), 9th (E), 11th (G)

Dm11
D Minor 11th

Middle C

F♯G♭ G♯A♭ A♯B♭   C♯D♭ D♯E♭   F♯G♭ G♯A♭ A♯B♭

2 **1** **1** **2** **4**

F G A B C D E F G A B

● use this note

1 2 3 4 or **5** use this finger

1 = thumb 2 = index finger 3 = middle finger 4 = ring finger 5 = little finger

Chord Spelling

1st (D), ♭3rd (F), 5th (A), ♭7th (C), 9th (E), 11th (G)

D11
D Dominant 11th

Middle C

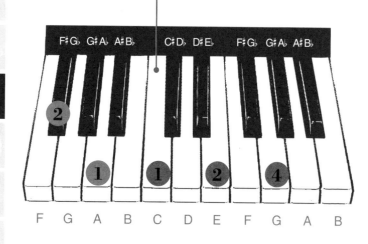

F G A B C D E F G A B

use this note

1 2 3 4 or **5** use this finger

1 = thumb   2 = index finger   3 = middle finger   4 = ring finger   5 = little finger

Chord Spelling

1st (D), 3rd (F#), 5th (A), ♭7th (C), 9th (E), 11th (G)

D11-9
D 11th Flattened 9th

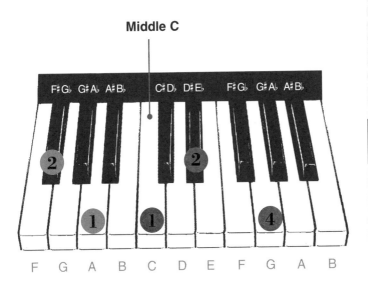

Middle C

F#G♭ G#A♭ A#B♭   C#D♭ D#E♭   F#G♭ G#A♭ A#B♭

F G A B C D E F G A B

use this note

1 2 3 4 or **5** use this finger

1 = thumb   2 = index finger   3 = middle finger   4 = ring finger   5 = little finger

Chord Spelling

1st (D), 3rd (F#), 5th (A), ♭7th (C), ♭9th (E♭), 11th (G)

Dmaj13
D Major 13th

Middle C

F#G♭ G#A♭ A#B♭   C#D♭ D#E♭   F#G♭ G#A♭ A#B♭

F G A B C D E F G A B

use this note

1 2 3 4 or **5**   use this finger

1 = thumb   2 = index finger   3 = middle finger   4 = ring finger   5 = little finger

Chord Spelling

1st (D), 3rd (F#), 5th (A), 7th (C#), 9th (E), 11th (G), 13th (B

Dm13
D Minor 13th

Middle C

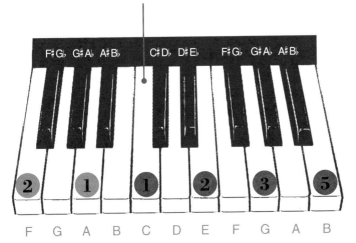

use this note

1 2 3 4 or **5** use this finger

1 = thumb 2 = index finger 3 = middle finger 4 = ring finger 5 = little finger

Chord Spelling

1st (D), ♭3rd (F), 5th (A), ♭7th (C), 9th (E), 11th (G), 13th (B)

D13
D Dominant 13th

Middle C

F#G♭ G#A♭ A#B♭ C#D♭ D#E♭ F#G♭ G#A♭ A#B♭

F G A B C D E F G A B

2 **1** **1** **2** **3** **5**

use this note

1 2 3 4 or **5** use this finger

1 = thumb 2 = index finger 3 = middle finger 4 = ring finger 5 = little finger

Chord Spelling

1st (D), 3rd (F#), 5th (A), ♭7th (C), 9th (E), 11th (G), 13th (B)

D13-9
D 13th Flattened 9th

Middle C

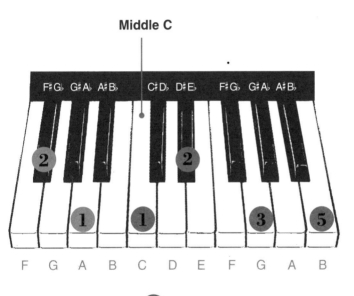

F G A B C D E F G A B

use this note

1 2 3 4 or **5** use this finger

1 = thumb 2 = index finger 3 = middle finger 4 = ring finger 5 = little finger

Chord Spelling

1st (D), 3rd (F♯), 5th (A), ♭7th (C), ♭9th (E♭), 11th (G), 13th (B)

E♭
E♭ Major

Middle C

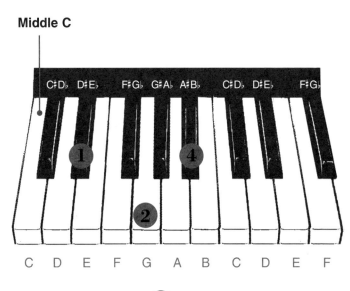

C D E F G A B C D E F

● use this note

1 2 3 4 or **5** use this finger

1 = thumb 2 = index finger 3 = middle finger 4 = ring finger 5 = little finger

Chord Spelling

1st (E♭), 3rd (G), 5th (B♭)

E♭m
E♭ Minor

Middle C

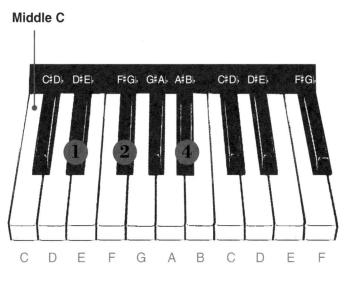

 use this note

1 2 3 4 or **5** use this finger

1 = thumb 2 = index finger 3 = middle finger 4 = ring finger 5 = little finger

Chord Spelling

1st (E♭), ♭3rd (G♭), 5th (B♭)

E♭+/E♭aug
E♭ Augmented Triad

Middle C

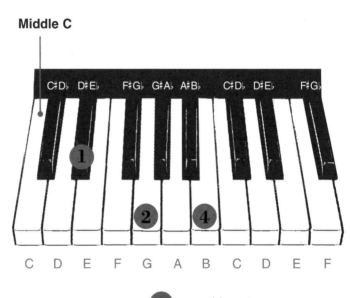

C D E F G A B C D E F

use this note

1 2 3 4 or **5** use this finger

1 = thumb   2 = index finger   3 = middle finger   4 = ring finger   5 = little finger

Chord Spelling

1st (E♭), 3rd (G), ♯5th (B)

E♭sus4
E♭ Suspended 4th

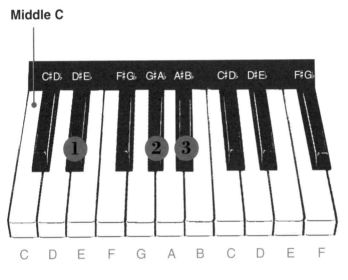

Middle C

C D E F G A B C D E F

🔘 use this note

1 2 3 4 or **5** use this finger

1 = thumb 2 = index finger 3 = middle finger 4 = ring finger 5 = little finger

Chord Spelling

1st (E♭), 4th (A♭), 5th (B♭)

E♭o/E♭dim
E♭ Diminished Triad

Middle C

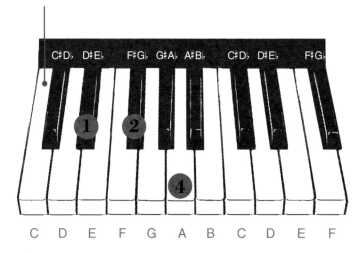

use this note

1 2 3 4 or **5** use this finger

1 = thumb   2 = index finger   3 = middle finger   4 = ring finger   5 = little finger

Chord Spelling

1st (E♭), ♭3rd (G♭), ♭5th (B♭♭)

E♭6
E♭ Major 6th

Middle C

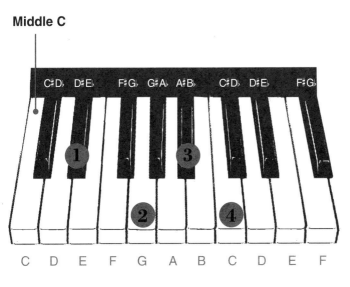

C D E F G A B C D E F

● use this note

1 2 3 4 or **5** use this finger

1 = thumb   2 = index finger   3 = middle finger   4 = ring finger   5 = little finger

Chord Spelling

1st (E♭), 3rd (G), 5th (B♭), 6th (C)

E♭m6
E♭ Minor 6th

Middle C

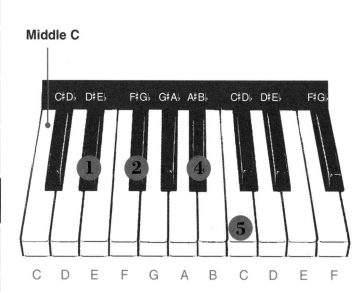

C♯D♭ D♯E♭   F♯G♭ G♯A♭ A♯B♭   C♯D♭ D♯E♭   F♯G♭

C   D   E   F   G   A   B   C   D   E   F

● use this note

1 2 3 4 or **5** use this finger

1 = thumb 2 = index finger 3 = middle finger 4 = ring finger 5 = little finger

Chord Spelling

1st (E♭), ♭3rd (G♭), 5th (B♭), 6th (C)

E♭maj7
E♭ Major 7th

Middle C

use this note

1 2 3 4 or **5** use this finger

1 = thumb   2 = index finger   3 = middle finger   4 = ring finger   5 = little finger

Chord Spelling

1st (E♭), 3rd (G), 5th (B♭), 7th (D)

E♭m7
E♭ Minor 7th

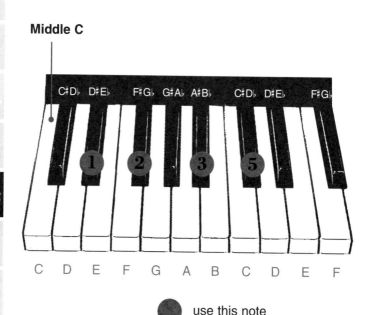

Middle C

C D E F G A B C D E F

🔵 use this note

1 2 3 4 or **5** use this finger

1 = thumb   2 = index finger   3 = middle finger   4 = ring finger   5 = little finger

Chord Spelling

1st (E♭), ♭3rd (G♭), 5th (B♭), ♭7th (D♭)

E♭7
E♭ Dominant 7th

A
B♭/A♯
B
C
C♯/D♭
D
E♭/D♯
E
F
F♯/G
G

Middle C

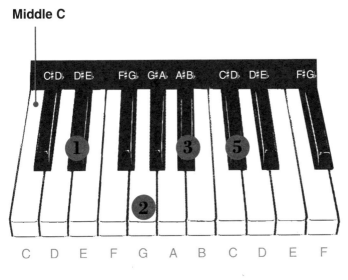

use this note

1 2 3 4 or **5** use this finger

1 = thumb 2 = index finger 3 = middle finger 4 = ring finger 5 = little finger

Chord Spelling

1st (E♭), 3rd (G), 5th (B♭), ♭7th (D♭)

E♭7sus4
E♭ Dominant 7th sus4

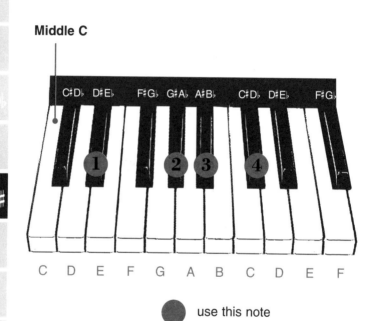

Middle C

use this note

1 2 3 4 or **5** use this finger

1 = thumb   2 = index finger   3 = middle finger   4 = ring finger   5 = little finger

Chord Spelling

1st (E♭), 4th (A♭), 5th (B♭), ♭7th (D♭)

E♭7+5
E♭ Dominant 7th
Augmented 5th

Middle C

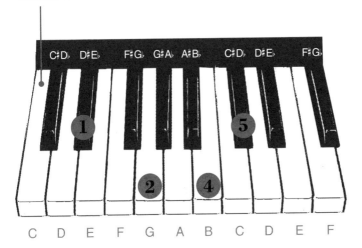

● use this note

1 2 3 4 or **5** use this finger

1 = thumb   2 = index finger   3 = middle finger   4 = ring finger   5 = little finger

Chord Spelling

1st (E♭), 3rd (G), #5th (B), ♭7th (D♭)

E♭7-5
E♭ Dominant 7th
Flattened 5th

Middle C

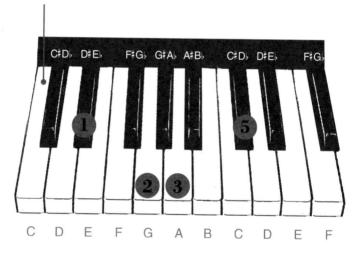

use this note

1 2 3 4 or **5** use this finger

1 = thumb   2 = index finger   3 = middle finger   4 = ring finger   5 = little finger

Chord Spelling

1st (E♭), 3rd (G), ♭5th (B♭♭), ♭7th (D♭)

E♭dim7
E♭ Diminished 7th

Middle C

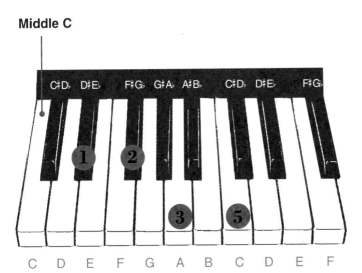

use this note

1 2 3 4 or **5** use this finger

1 = thumb 2 = index finger 3 = middle finger 4 = ring finger 5 = little finger

Chord Spelling

1st (E♭), ♭3rd (G♭), ♭5th (B♭♭), ♭♭7th (D♭♭)

E♭m7-5
E♭ Minor 7th
Flattened 5th

Middle C

C♯D♭ D♯E♭   F♯G♭ G♯A♭ A♯B♭   C♯D♭ D♯E♭   F♯G♭

C D E F G A B C D E F

● use this note

1 2 3 4 or **5** use this finger

1 = thumb   2 = index finger   3 = middle finger   4 = ring finger   5 = little finger

Chord Spelling

1st (E♭), ♭3rd (G♭), ♭5th (B♭♭), ♭7th (D♭)

E♭mmaj7
E♭ Minor-Major 7th

Middle C

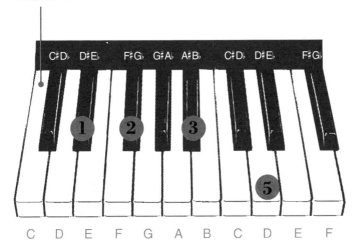

use this note

1 2 3 4 or **5** use this finger

1 = thumb 2 = index finger 3 = middle finger 4 = ring finger 5 = little finger

Chord Spelling

1st (E♭), ♭3rd (G♭), 5th (B♭), 7th (D)

E♭maj9
E♭ Major 9th

Middle C

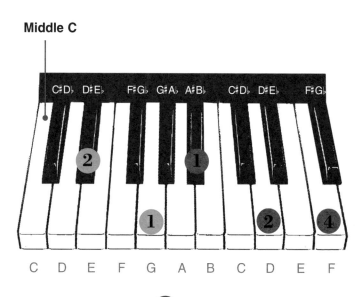

use this note

1 2 3 4 or **5** use this finger

1 = thumb　2 = index finger　3 = middle finger　4 = ring finger　5 = little finger

Chord Spelling

1st (E♭), 3rd (G), 5th (B♭), 7th (D), 9th (F)

E♭m9
E♭ Minor 9th

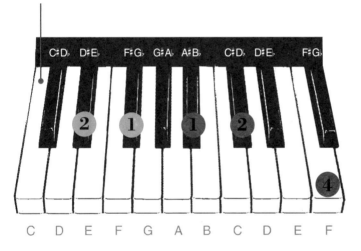

Middle C

use this note

1 2 3 4 or **5** use this finger

1 = thumb 2 = index finger 3 = middle finger 4 = ring finger 5 = little finger

Chord Spelling

1st (E♭), ♭3rd (G♭), 5th (B♭), ♭7th (D♭), 9th (F)

E♭9
E♭ Dominant 9th

Middle C

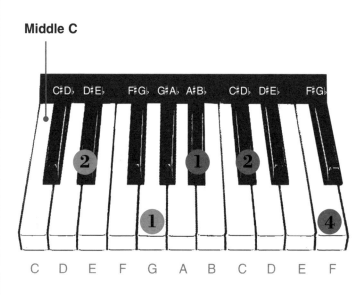

C D E F G A B C D E F

● use this note

1 2 3 4 or **5** use this finger

1 = thumb 2 = index finger 3 = middle finger 4 = ring finger 5 = little finger

Chord Spelling

1st (E♭), 3rd (G), 5th (B♭), ♭7th (D♭), 9th (F)

E♭9+5
E♭ 9th Augmented 5th

Middle C

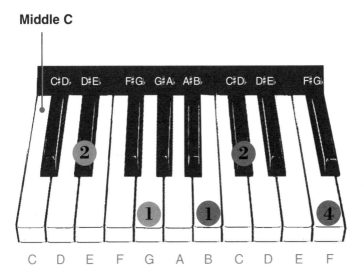

use this note

1 2 3 4 or **5** use this finger

1 = thumb 2 = index finger 3 = middle finger 4 = ring finger 5 = little finger

Chord Spelling

1st (E♭), 3rd (G), ♯5th (B), ♭7th (D♭), 9th (F)

E♭9-5
E♭ 9th Flattened 5th

Middle C

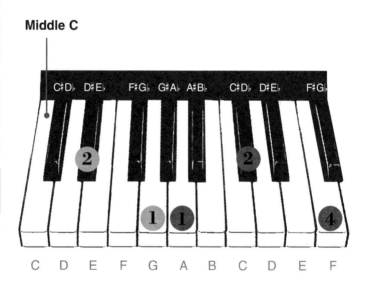

C D E F G A B C D E F

● use this note

1 2 3 4 or **5** use this finger

1 = thumb   2 = index finger   3 = middle finger   4 = ring finger   5 = little finger

Chord Spelling

1st (E♭), 3rd (G), ♭5th (B♭♭), ♭7th (D♭), 9th (F)

E♭9/6
E♭ 9th Add 6th

Middle C

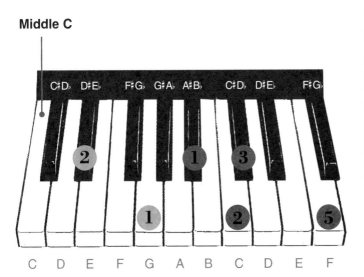

use this note

1 2 3 4 or 5 use this finger

1 = thumb 2 = index finger 3 = middle finger 4 = ring finger 5 = little finger

Chord Spelling

1st (E♭), 3rd (G), 5th (B♭), 6th (C), ♭7th (D♭), 9th (F)

E♭maj11
E♭ Major 11th

Middle C

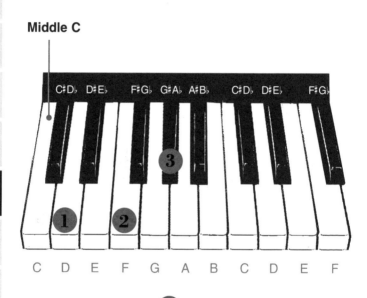

use this note

1 2 3 4 or **5** use this finger

1 = thumb   2 = index finger   3 = middle finger   4 = ring finger   5 = little finger

Chord Spelling

1st (E♭), 3rd (G), 5th (B♭), 7th (D), 9th (F), 11th (A♭)

E♭m11
E♭ Minor 11th

Middle C

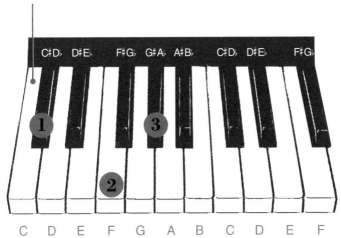

C D E F G A B C D E F

use this note

1 2 3 4 or **5** use this finger

1 = thumb 2 = index finger 3 = middle finger 4 = ring finger 5 = little finger

Chord Spelling

1st (E♭), ♭3rd (G♭), 5th (B♭), ♭7th (D♭), 9th (F), 11th (A♭)

E♭11
E♭ Dominant 11th

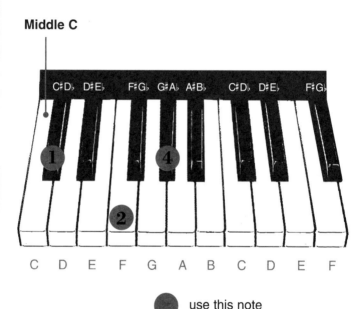

Middle C

C D E F G A B C D E F

use this note

1 2 3 4 or **5** use this finger

1 = thumb 2 = index finger 3 = middle finger 4 = ring finger 5 = little finger

Chord Spelling

1st (E♭), 3rd (G), 5th (B♭), ♭7th (D♭), 9th (F), 11th (A♭)

E♭11-9
E♭ 11th Flattened 9th

Middle C

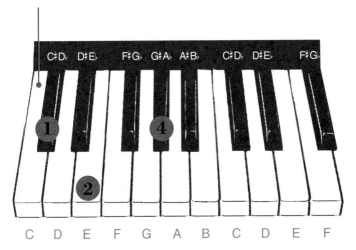

C D E F G A B C D E F

● use this note

1 2 3 4 or **5** use this finger

1 = thumb 2 = index finger 3 = middle finger 4 = ring finger 5 = little finger

Chord Spelling

1st (E♭), 3rd (G), 5th (B♭), ♭7th (D♭), ♭9th (F♭), 11th (A♭)

4 **2** **1**

E♭maj13
E♭ Major 13th

Middle C

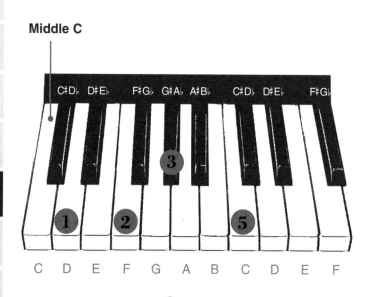

use this note

1 2 3 4 or **5** use this finger

1 = thumb 2 = index finger 3 = middle finger 4 = ring finger 5 = little finger

Chord Spelling

1st (E♭), 3rd (G), 5th (B♭), 7th (D), 9th (F), 11th (A♭), 13th (C)

E♭m13
E♭ Minor 13th

Middle C

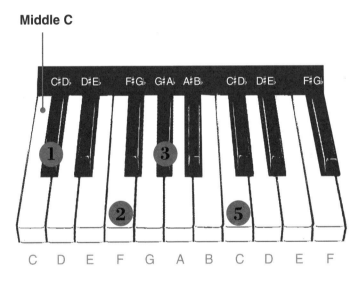

use this note

1 2 3 4 or **5** use this finger

1 = thumb 2 = index finger 3 = middle finger 4 = ring finger 5 = little finger

Chord Spelling

1st (E♭), ♭3rd (G♭), 5th (B♭), ♭7th (D♭), 9th (F), 11th (A♭), 13th (C)

E♭13
E♭ Dominant 13th

Middle C

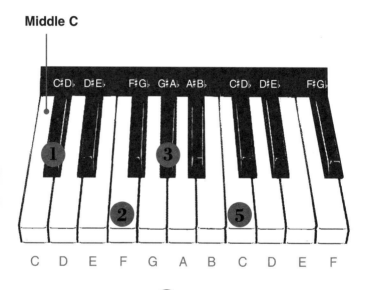

C D E F G A B C D E F

use this note

1 2 3 4 or **5** use this finger

1 = thumb 2 = index finger 3 = middle finger 4 = ring finger 5 = little finger

Chord Spelling

1st (E♭), 3rd (G), 5th (B♭), ♭7th (D♭), 9th (F), 11th (A♭), 13th (C)

E♭13-9
E♭ 13th Flattened 9th

Middle C

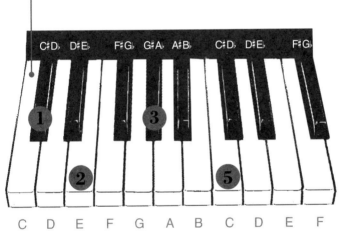

C D E F G A B C D E F

use this note

1 2 3 4 or **5** use this finger

1 = thumb   2 = index finger   3 = middle finger   4 = ring finger   5 = little finger

Chord Spelling

st (E♭), 3rd (G), 5th (B♭), ♭7th (D♭), ♭9th (F♭), 11th (A♭), 13th (C)

E
E Major

Middle C

C♯D♭ D♯E♭　F♯G♭ G♯A♭ A♯B♭　C♯D♭ D♯E♭　F♯G♭

C D E F G A B C D E F

 use this note

1 2 3 4 or **5** use this finger

1 = thumb　2 = index finger　3 = middle finger　4 = ring finger　5 = little finger

Chord Spelling

1st (E), 3rd (G♯), 5th (B)

Em
E Minor

Middle C

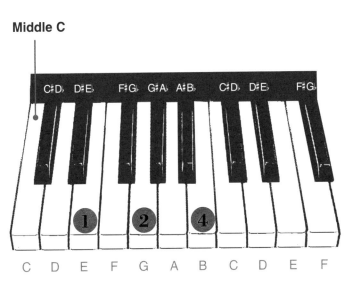

C D E F G A B C D E F

🔴 use this note

1 2 3 4 or **5** use this finger

1 = thumb 2 = index finger 3 = middle finger 4 = ring finger 5 = little finger

Chord Spelling

1st (E), ♭3rd (G), 5th (B)

E+/Eaug
E Augmented Triad

Middle C

C#D♭ D#E♭ F#G♭ G#A♭ A#B♭ C#D♭ D#E♭ F#G♭

C D E F G A B C D E F

● use this note

1 2 3 4 or **5** use this finger

1 = thumb   2 = index finger   3 = middle finger   4 = ring finger   5 = little finger

Chord Spelling

1st (E), 3rd (G#), #5th (B#)

Esus4
E Suspended 4th

Middle C

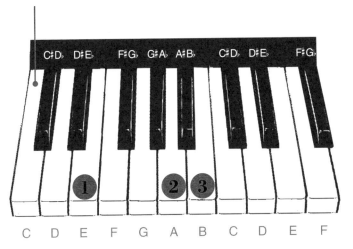

use this note

1 2 3 4 or **5** use this finger

1 = thumb 2 = index finger 3 = middle finger 4 = ring finger 5 = little finger

Chord Spelling

1st (E), 4th (A), 5th (B)

Eo/Edim
E Diminished Triad

Middle C

C D E F G A B C D E F

use this note

1 2 3 4 or **5** use this finger

1 = thumb 2 = index finger 3 = middle finger 4 = ring finger 5 = little finger

Chord Spelling

1st (E), ♭3rd (G), ♭5th (B♭)

E6
E Major 6th

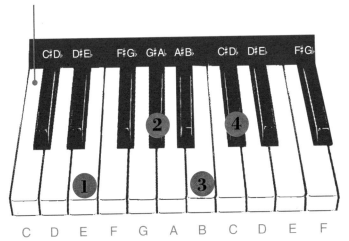

Middle C

C#D♭ D#E♭   F#G♭ G#A♭ A#B♭   C#D♭ D#E♭   F#G♭

C D E F G A B C D E F

● use this note

1 2 3 4 or **5** use this finger

1 = thumb 2 = index finger 3 = middle finger 4 = ring finger 5 = little finger

Chord Spelling

1st (E), 3rd (G#), 5th (B), 6th (C#)

Em6
E Minor 6th

Middle C

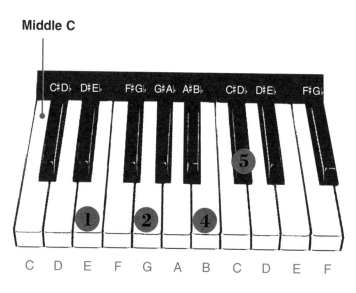

use this note

1 2 3 4 or **5** use this finger

1 = thumb 2 = index finger 3 = middle finger 4 = ring finger 5 = little finger

Chord Spelling

1st (E), ♭3rd (G), 5th (B), 6th (C♯)

Emaj7
E Major 7th

Middle C

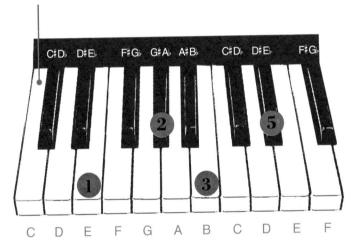

 use this note

1 2 3 4 or **5** use this finger

1 = thumb   2 = index finger   3 = middle finger   4 = ring finger   5 = little finger

Chord Spelling

1st (E), 3rd (G#), 5th (B), 7th (D#)

Em7
E Minor 7th

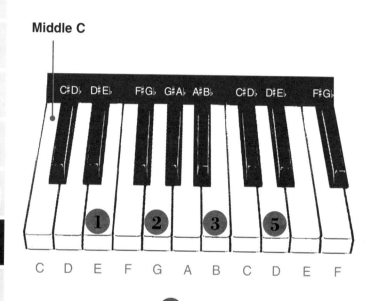

Middle C

C♯D♭ D♯E♭   F♯G♭ G♯A♭ A♯B♭   C♯D♭ D♯E♭   F♯G♭

C D E F G A B C D E F

1 **2** **3** **5**

⬤ use this note

1 2 3 4 or **5** use this finger

1 = thumb   2 = index finger   3 = middle finger   4 = ring finger   5 = little finger

Chord Spelling

1st (E), ♭3rd (G), 5th (B), ♭7th (D)

E7
E Dominant 7th

Middle C

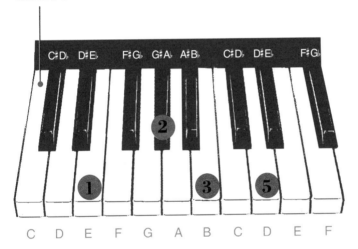

use this note

1 2 3 4 or **5** use this finger

1 = thumb 2 = index finger 3 = middle finger 4 = ring finger 5 = little finger

Chord Spelling

1st (E), 3rd (G#), 5th (B), ♭7th (D)

E7sus4
E Dominant 7th sus4

Middle C

C♯D♭　D♯E♭　　F♯G♭　G♯A♭　A♯B♭　　C♯D♭　D♯E♭　　F♯G♭

C　D　E　F　G　A　B　C　D　E　F

use this note

1 2 3 4 or **5** use this finger

1 = thumb　2 = index finger　3 = middle finger　4 = ring finger　5 = little finger

Chord Spelling

1st (E), 4th (A), 5th (B), ♭7th (D)

E7+5
E Dominant 7th
Augmented 5th

Middle C

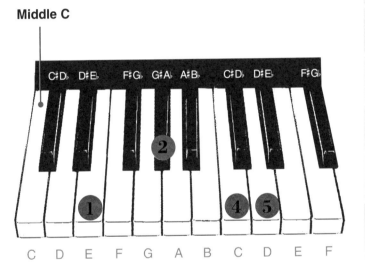

use this note

1 2 3 4 or **5** use this finger

1 = thumb   2 = index finger   3 = middle finger   4 = ring finger   5 = little finger

Chord Spelling

1st (E), 3rd (G♯), ♯5th (B♯), ♭7th (D)

E7-5
E Dominant 7th
Flattened 5th

Middle C

use this note

1 2 3 4 or **5** use this finger

1 = thumb 2 = index finger 3 = middle finger 4 = ring finger 5 = little finger

Chord Spelling

1st (E), 3rd (G#), ♭5th (B♭), ♭7th (D)

Edim7
E Diminished 7th

Middle C

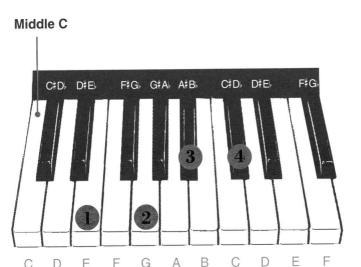

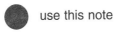
use this note

1 2 3 4 or **5** use this finger

1 = thumb **2** = index finger **3** = middle finger **4** = ring finger **5** = little finger

Chord Spelling

1st (E), ♭3rd (G), ♭5th (B♭), ♭♭7th (D♭)

Em7-5
E Minor 7th
Flattened 5th

Middle C

use this note

1 2 3 4 or **5** use this finger

1 = thumb   2 = index finger   3 = middle finger   4 = ring finger   5 = little finger

Chord Spelling

1st (E), ♭3rd (G), ♭5th (B♭), ♭7th (D)

Emmaj7
E Minor-Major 7th

Middle C

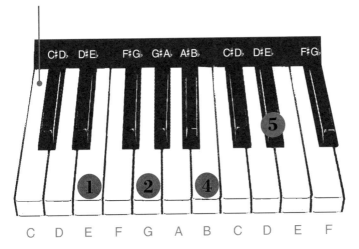

C D E F G A B C D E F

use this note

1 2 3 4 or **5** use this finger

1 = thumb 2 = index finger 3 = middle finger 4 = ring finger 5 = little finger

Chord Spelling

1st (E), ♭3rd (G), 5th (B), 7th (D♯)

E

Emaj9
E Major 9th

Middle C

C♯D♭ D♯E♭   F♯G♭ G♯A♭ A♯B♭   C♯D♭ D♯E♭   F♯G♭

C D E F G A B C D E F

use this note

1 2 3 4 or **5** use this finger

1 = thumb 2 = index finger 3 = middle finger 4 = ring finger 5 = little finger

Chord Spelling

1st (E), 3rd (G♯), 5th (B), 7th (D♯), 9th (F♯)

Em9
E Minor 9th

Middle C

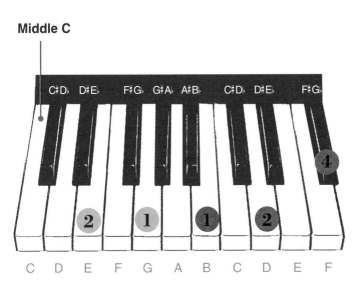

 use this note

1 2 3 4 or **5** use this finger

1 = thumb 2 = index finger 3 = middle finger 4 = ring finger 5 = little finger

Chord Spelling

1st (E), ♭3rd (G), 5th (B), ♭7th (D), 9th (F♯)

E9
E Dominant 9th

Middle C

C D E F G A B C D E F

 use this note

1 2 3 4 or **5** use this finger

1 = thumb **2** = index finger **3** = middle finger **4** = ring finger **5** = little finger

Chord Spelling

1st (E), 3rd (G#), 5th (B), ♭7th (D), 9th (F#)

E9+5
E 9th Augmented 5th

Middle C

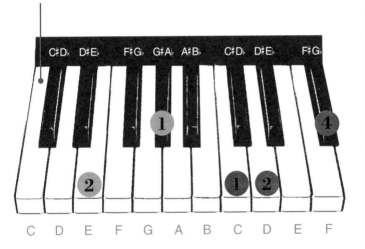

C D E F G A B C D E F

use this note

1 2 3 4 or **5** use this finger

1 = thumb   2 = index finger   3 = middle finger   4 = ring finger   5 = little finger

Chord Spelling

1st (E), 3rd (G#), #5th (B#), ♭7th (D), 9th (F#)

E9-5
E 9th Flattened 5th

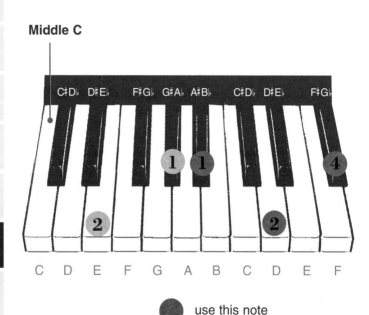

Middle C

use this note

1 2 3 4 or **5** use this finger

1 = thumb   2 = index finger   3 = middle finger   4 = ring finger   5 = little finger

Chord Spelling

1st (E), 3rd (G♯), ♭5th (B♭), ♭7th (D), 9th (F♯)

E9/6
E 9th Add 6th

Middle C

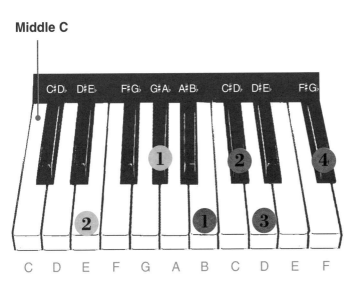

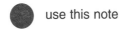 use this note

1 2 3 4 or **5** use this finger

1 = thumb 2 = index finger 3 = middle finger 4 = ring finger 5 = little finger

Chord Spelling

1st (E), 3rd (G♯), 5th (B), 6th (C♯), ♭7th (D), 9th (F♯)

Emaj11
E Major 11th

Middle C

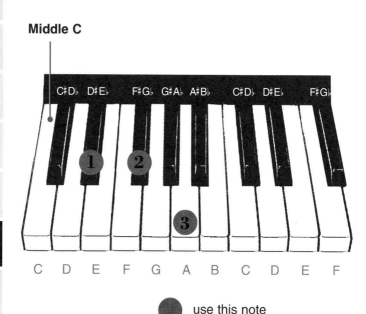

C D E F G A B C D E F

● use this note

1 2 3 4 or **5** use this finger

1 = thumb   2 = index finger   3 = middle finger   4 = ring finger   5 = little finger

Chord Spelling

1st (E), 3rd (G#), 5th (B), 7th (D#), 9th (F#), 11th (A)

Em11
E Minor 11th

Middle C

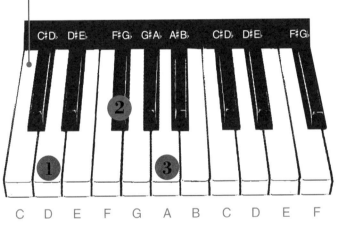

C#D♭ D#E♭   F#G♭ G#A♭ A#B♭   C#D♭ D#E♭   F#G♭

C D E F G A B C D E F

● use this note

1 2 3 4 or **5** use this finger

1 = thumb 2 = index finger 3 = middle finger 4 = ring finger 5 = little finger

Chord Spelling

1st (E), ♭3rd (G), 5th (B), ♭7th (D), 9th (F#), 11th (A)

E11
E Dominant 11th

Middle C

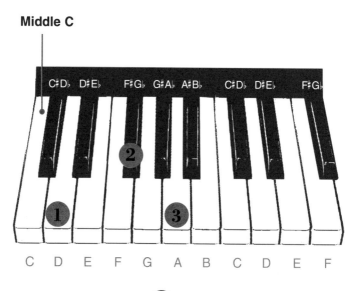

C D E F G A B C D E F

 use this note

1 2 3 4 or **5** use this finger

1 = thumb   2 = index finger   3 = middle finger   4 = ring finger   5 = little finger

Chord Spelling

1st (E), 3rd (G#), 5th (B), ♭7th (D), 9th (F#), 11th (A)

E11-9
E 11th Flattened 9th

Middle C

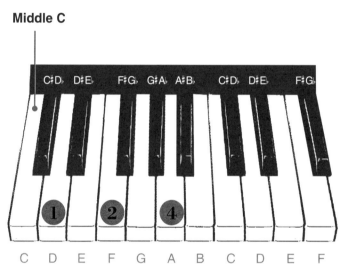

 use this note

1 2 3 4 or **5** use this finger

1 = thumb   2 = index finger   3 = middle finger   4 = ring finger   5 = little finger

Chord Spelling

1st (E), 3rd (G#), 5th (B), ♭7th (D), ♭9th (F), 11th (A)

Emaj13
E Major 13th

Middle C

C D E F G A B C D E F

use this note

1 2 3 4 or **5** use this finger

1 = thumb   2 = index finger   3 = middle finger   4 = ring finger   5 = little finger

Chord Spelling

1st (E), 3rd (G#), 5th (B), 7th (D#), 9th (F#), 11th (A), 13th (C

Em13
E Minor 13th

Middle C

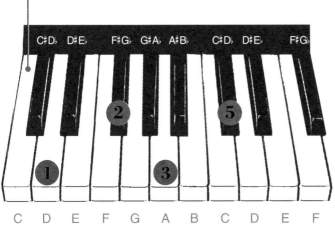

C#D♭ D#E♭   F#G♭ G#A♭ A#B♭   C#D♭ D#E♭   F#G♭

C D E F G A B C D E F

use this note

1 2 3 4 or **5** use this finger

1 = thumb 2 = index finger 3 = middle finger 4 = ring finger 5 = little finger

Chord Spelling

1st (E), ♭3rd (G), 5th (B), ♭7th (D), 9th (F#), 11th (A), 13th (C#)

A
B♭/A#
B
C
C#/D♭
D
E♭/D#
E
F
F#/G♭
G
A♭/G#

E13
E Dominant 13th

Middle C

C#D♭ D#E♭   F#G♭ G#A♭ A#B♭   C#D♭ D#E♭   F#G♭

C D E F G A B C D E F

● use this note

1 2 3 4 or **5** use this finger

1 = thumb 2 = index finger 3 = middle finger 4 = ring finger 5 = little finger

Chord Spelling

1st (E), 3rd (G♯), 5th (B), ♭7th (D), 9th (F♯), 11th (A), 13th (C

E13-9
E 13th Flattened 9th

Middle C

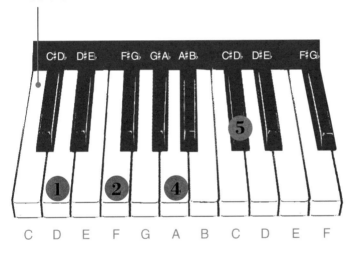

C D E F G A B C D E F

● use this note

1 2 3 4 or **5** use this finger

1 = thumb 2 = index finger 3 = middle finger 4 = ring finger 5 = little finger

Chord Spelling

1st (E), 3rd (G♯), 5th (B), ♭7th (D), ♭9th (F), 11th (A), 13th (C♯)

E

F
F Major

Middle C

C♯D♭ D♯E♭ F♯G♭ G♯A♭ A♯B♭ C♯D♭ D♯E♭ F♯G♭

① ② ④

C D E F G A B C D E F

● use this note

1 2 3 4 or **5** use this finger

1 = thumb 2 = index finger 3 = middle finger 4 = ring finger 5 = little finger

Chord Spelling

1st (F), 3rd (A), 5th (C)

A B♭/A♯ B C C♯/D♭ D E♭/D♯ E **F** F♯/G♭ G A♭/G♯

Fm
F Minor

Middle C

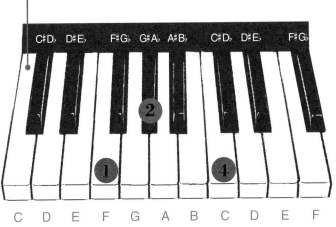

use this note

1 2 3 4 or **5** use this finger

1 = thumb   2 = index finger   3 = middle finger   4 = ring finger   5 = little finger

Chord Spelling

1st (F), ♭3rd (A♭), 5th (C)

F+/Faug
F Augmented Triad

Middle C

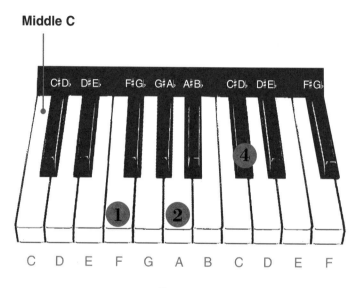

C D E F G A B C D E F

use this note

1 2 3 4 or **5** use this finger

1 = thumb 2 = index finger 3 = middle finger 4 = ring finger 5 = little finger

Chord Spelling

1st (F), 3rd (A), ♯5th (C♯)

Fsus4
F Suspended 4th

Middle C

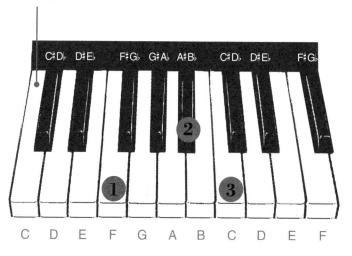

C♯D♭ D♯E♭ F♯G♭ G♯A♭ A♯B♭ C♯D♭ D♯E♭ F♯G♭

C D E F G A B C D E F

● use this note

1 2 3 4 or **5** use this finger

1 = thumb 2 = index finger 3 = middle finger 4 = ring finger 5 = little finger

Chord Spelling

1st (F), 4th (B♭), 5th (C)

A

B♭/A♯

B

C

C♯/D♭

D

E♭/D♯

E

F

F♯/G♭

G

A♭/G♯

Fo/Fdim
F Diminished Triad

Middle C

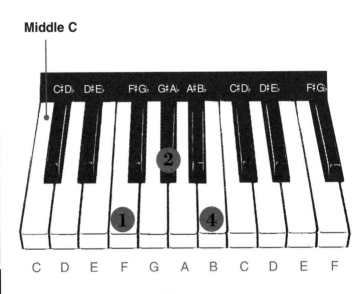

C D E F G A B C D E F

● use this note

1 2 3 4 or **5** use this finger

1 = thumb 2 = index finger 3 = middle finger 4 = ring finger 5 = little finger

Chord Spelling

1st (F), ♭3rd (A♭), ♭5th (C♭)

F6
F Major 6th

Middle C

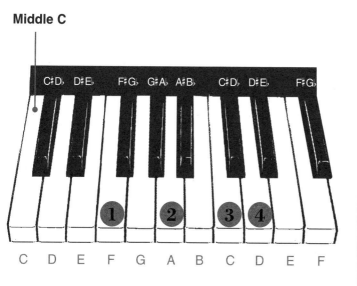

use this note

1 2 3 4 or **5** use this finger

1 = thumb   2 = index finger   3 = middle finger   4 = ring finger   5 = little finger

Chord Spelling

1st (F), 3rd (A), 5th (C), 6th (D)

Fm6
F Minor 6th

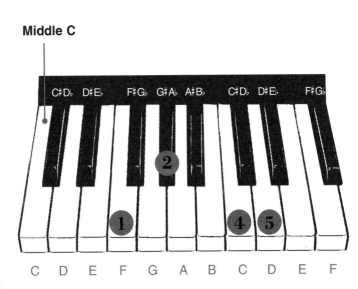

Middle C

C D E F G A B C D E F

● use this note

1 2 3 4 or **5** use this finger

1 = thumb 2 = index finger 3 = middle finger 4 = ring finger 5 = little finger

Chord Spelling

1st (F), ♭3rd (A♭), 5th (C), 6th (D)

Fmaj7
F Major 7th

Middle C

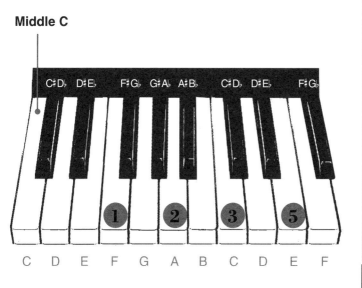

use this note

1 2 3 4 or **5** use this finger

1 = thumb 2 = index finger 3 = middle finger 4 = ring finger 5 = little finger

Chord Spelling

1st (F), 3rd (A), 5th (C), 7th (E)

Fm7
F Minor 7th

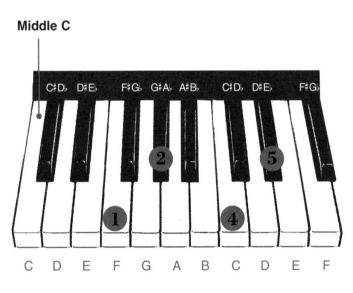

Middle C

C#D♭ D#E♭   F#G♭ G#A♭ A#B♭   C#D♭ D#E♭   F#G♭

C D E F G A B C D E F

use this note

1 2 3 4 or **5** use this finger

1 = thumb 2 = index finger 3 = middle finger 4 = ring finger 5 = little finger

Chord Spelling

1st (F), ♭3rd (A♭), 5th (C), ♭7th (E♭)

F7
F Dominant 7th

Middle C

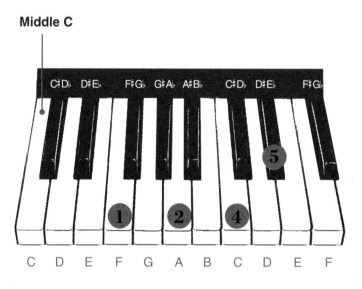

use this note

1 2 3 4 or **5** use this finger

1 = thumb 2 = index finger 3 = middle finger 4 = ring finger 5 = little finger

Chord Spelling

1st (F), 3rd (A), 5th (C), ♭7th (E♭)

F7sus4
F Dominant 7th sus4

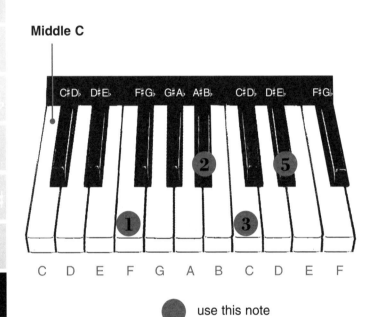

Middle C

C#D♭ D#E♭ F#G♭ G#A♭ A#B♭ C#D♭ D#E♭ F#G♭

C D E F G A B C D E F

● use this note

1 2 3 4 or **5** use this finger

1 = thumb 2 = index finger 3 = middle finger 4 = ring finger 5 = little finger

Chord Spelling

1st (F), 4th (B♭), 5th (C), ♭7th (E♭)

F7+5
F Dominant 7th
Augmented 5th

Middle C

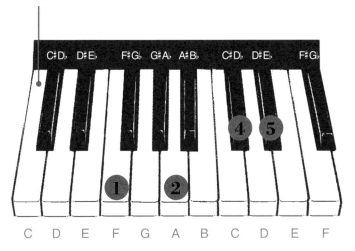

C D E F G A B C D E F

use this note

1 2 3 4 or **5** use this finger

1 = thumb   2 = index finger   3 = middle finger   4 = ring finger   5 = little finger

Chord Spelling

1st (F), 3rd (A), #5th (C#), ♭7th (E♭)

F7-5
F Dominant 7th
Flattened 5th

Middle C

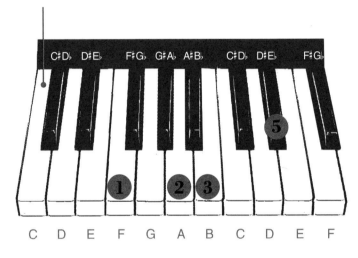

C D E F G A B C D E F

use this note

1 2 3 4 or **5** use this finger

1 = thumb 2 = index finger 3 = middle finger 4 = ring finger 5 = little finger

Chord Spelling

1st (F), 3rd (A), ♭5th (C♭), ♭7th (E♭)

Fdim7
F Diminished 7th

Middle C

C#Db D#Eb   F#Gb G#Ab A#Bb   C#Db D#Eb   F#Gb

C   D   E   F   G   A   B   C   D   E   F

🔴 use this note

1 2 3 4 or **5** use this finger

1 = thumb   2 = index finger   3 = middle finger   4 = ring finger   5 = little finger

Chord Spelling

1st (F), ♭3rd (A♭), ♭5th (C♭), ♭♭7th (E♭♭)

Fm7-5
F Minor 7th
Flattened 5th

Middle C

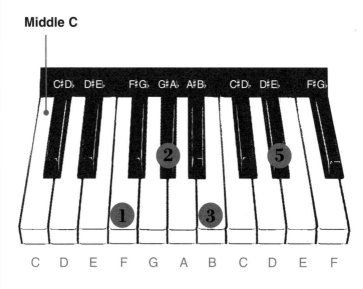

use this note

1 2 3 4 or **5**   use this finger

1 = thumb   2 = index finger   3 = middle finger   4 = ring finger   5 = little finger

Chord Spelling

1st (F), ♭3rd (A♭), ♭5th (C♭), ♭7th (E♭)

Fmmaj7
F Minor-Major 7th

Middle C

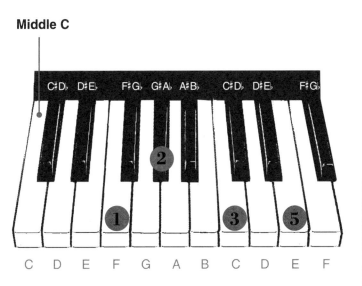

C D E F G A B C D E F

● use this note

1 2 3 4 or **5** use this finger

1 = thumb 2 = index finger 3 = middle finger 4 = ring finger 5 = little finger

Chord Spelling

1st (F), ♭3rd (A♭), 5th (C), 7th (E)

Fmaj9
F Major 9th

Middle C

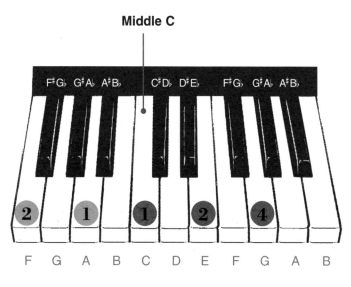

F♯G♭ G♯A♭ A♯B♭   C♯D♭ D♯E♭   F♯G♭ G♯A♭ A♯B♭

2   **1**   **1**   **2**   **4**

F G A B C D E F G A B

use this note

1 2 3 4 or **5**   use this finger

1 = thumb   2 = index finger   3 = middle finger   4 = ring finger   5 = little finger

Chord Spelling

1st (F), 3rd (A), 5th (C), 7th (E), 9th (G)

Fm9
F Minor 9th

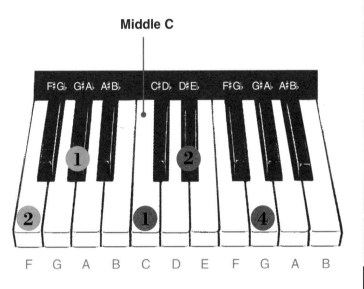

Middle C

F♯G♭ G♯A♭ A♯B♭   C♯D♭ D♯E♭   F♯G♭ G♯A♭ A♯B♭

F G A B C D E F G A B

● use this note

1 2 3 4 or **5** use this finger

1 = thumb   2 = index finger   3 = middle finger   4 = ring finger   5 = little finger

Chord Spelling

1st (F), ♭3rd (A♭), 5th (C), ♭7th (E♭), 9th (G)

F9
F Dominant 9th

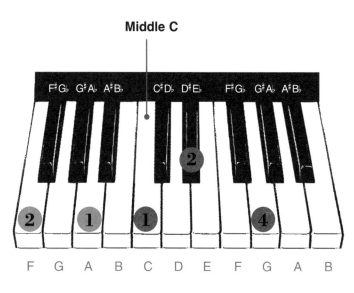

Middle C

F#G♭ G#A♭ A#B♭   C#D♭ D#E♭   F#G♭ G#A♭ A#B♭

F G A B C D E F G A B

2 **1** **1** **2** **4**

use this note

1 2 3 4 or **5**   use this finger

1 = thumb   2 = index finger   3 = middle finger   4 = ring finger   5 = little finger

Chord Spelling

1st (F), 3rd (A), 5th (C), ♭7th (E♭), 9th (G)

F9+5
F 9th Augmented 5th

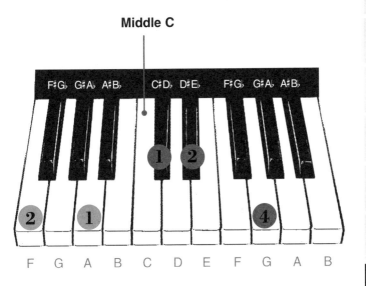

Middle C

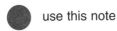 use this note

1 2 3 4 or **5** use this finger

1 = thumb 2 = index finger 3 = middle finger 4 = ring finger 5 = little finger

Chord Spelling

1st (F), 3rd (A), ♯5th (C♯), ♭7th (E♭), 9th (G)

F9-5
F 9th Flattened 5th

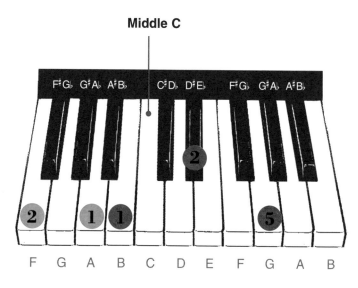

Middle C

F♯G♭ G♯A♭ A♯B♭   C♯D♭ D♯E♭   F♯G♭ G♯A♭ A♯B♭

F G A B C D E F G A B

use this note

1 2 3 4 or **5** use this finger

1 = thumb   2 = index finger   3 = middle finger   4 = ring finger   5 = little finger

Chord Spelling

1st (F), 3rd (A), ♭5th (C♭), ♭7th (E♭), 9th (G)

F9/6
F 9th Add 6th

Middle C

use this note

1 2 3 4 or **5** use this finger

1 = thumb 2 = index finger 3 = middle finger 4 = ring finger 5 = little finger

Chord Spelling

1st (F), 3rd (A), 5th (C), 6th (D), ♭7th (E♭), 9th (G)

Fmaj11
F Major 11th

Middle C

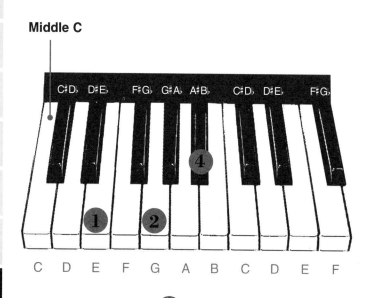

C D E F G A B C D E F

use this note

1 2 3 4 or **5** use this finger

1 = thumb 2 = index finger 3 = middle finger 4 = ring finger 5 = little finger

Chord Spelling

1st (F), 3rd (A), 5th (C), 7th (E), 9th (G), 11th (B♭)

Fm11
F Minor 11th

Middle C

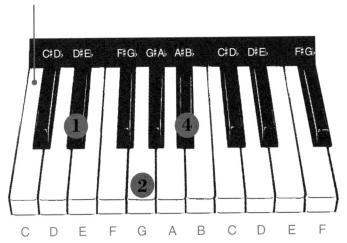

C♯D♭ D♯E♭ F♯G♭ G♯A♭ A♯B♭ C♯D♭ D♯E♭ F♯G♭

C D E F G A B C D E F

 use this note

1 2 3 4 or **5** use this finger

1 = thumb 2 = index finger 3 = middle finger 4 = ring finger 5 = little finger

Chord Spelling

1st (F), ♭3rd (A♭), 5th (C), ♭7th (E♭), 9th (G), 11th (B♭)

F11
F Dominant 11th

Middle C

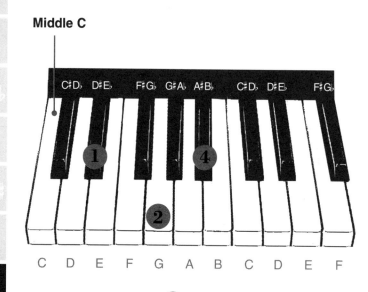

use this note

1 2 3 4 or **5** use this finger

1 = thumb   2 = index finger   3 = middle finger   4 = ring finger   5 = little finger

Chord Spelling

1st (F), 3rd (A), 5th (C), ♭7th (E♭), 9th (G), 11th (B♭)

F11-9
F 11th Flattened 9th

Middle C

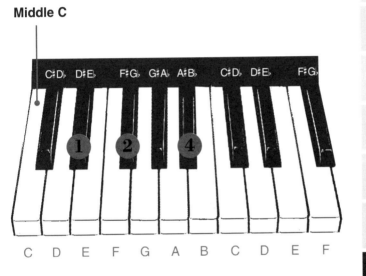

🔴 use this note

1 2 3 4 or **5** use this finger

1 = thumb   2 = index finger   3 = middle finger   4 = ring finger   5 = little finger

Chord Spelling

1st (F), 3rd (A), 5th (C), ♭7th (E♭), ♭9th (G♭), 11th (B♭)

4   **2**   **1**

Fmaj13
F Major 13th

Middle C

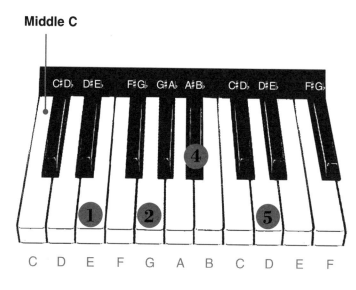

C D E F G A B C D E F

use this note

1 2 3 4 or **5** use this finger

1 = thumb 2 = index finger 3 = middle finger 4 = ring finger 5 = little finger

Chord Spelling

1st (F), 3rd (A), 5th (C), 7th (E), 9th (G), 11th (B♭), 13th (D)

Fm13
F Minor 13th

Middle C

C#D♭ D#E♭ F#G♭ G#A♭ A#B♭ C#D♭ D#E♭ F#G♭

C D E F G A B C D E F

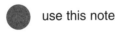 use this note

1 2 3 4 or **5** use this finger

1 = thumb   2 = index finger   3 = middle finger   4 = ring finger   5 = little finger

Chord Spelling

1st (F), ♭3rd (A♭), 5th (C), ♭7th (E♭), 9th (G), 11th (B♭), 13th (D)

F13
F Dominant 13th

Middle C

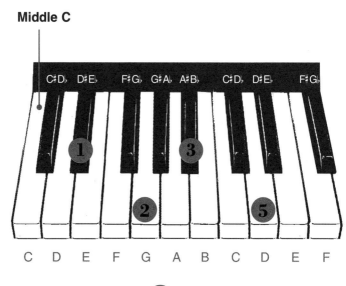

C#D♭ D#E♭ F#G♭ G#A♭ A#B♭ C#D♭ D#E♭ F#G♭

C D E F G A B C D E F

use this note

1 2 3 4 or **5** use this finger

1 = thumb   2 = index finger   3 = middle finger   4 = ring finger   5 = little finger

Chord Spelling

1st (F), 3rd (A), 5th (C), ♭7th (E♭), 9th (G), 11th (B♭), 13th (D)

 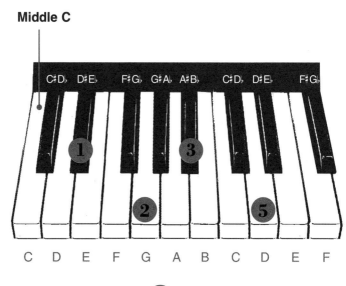

F13-9
F 13th Flattened 9th

Middle C

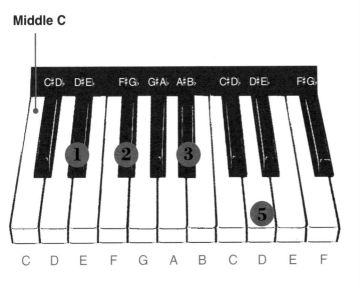

C D E F G A B C D E F

use this note

1 2 3 4 or **5** use this finger

1 = thumb 2 = index finger 3 = middle finger 4 = ring finger 5 = little finger

Chord Spelling

t (F), 3rd (A), 5th (C), ♭7th (E♭), ♭9th (G♭), 11th (B♭), 13th (D)

F♯ Major

Middle C

F♯G♭ G♯A♭ A♯B♭   C♯D♭ D♯E♭   F♯G♭ G♯A♭ A♯B♭

F G A B C D E F G A B

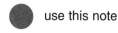 use this note

1 2 3 4 or **5** use this finger

1 = thumb   2 = index finger   3 = middle finger   4 = ring finger   5 = little finger

Chord Spelling

1st (F♯), 3rd (A♯), 5th (C♯)

F#m
F# Minor

Middle C

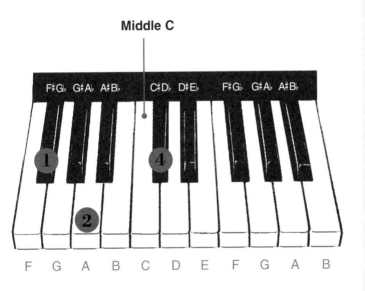

F#G♭ G#A♭ A#B♭   C#D♭ D#E♭   F#G♭ G#A♭ A#B♭

F G A B C D E F G A B

use this note

1 2 3 4 or **5** use this finger

1 = thumb 2 = index finger 3 = middle finger 4 = ring finger 5 = little finger

Chord Spelling

1st (F#), ♭3rd (A), 5th (C#)

F#+/F#aug
F# Augmented Triad

Middle C

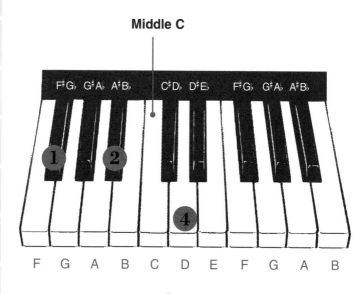

F G A B C D E F G A B

⬤ use this note

1 2 3 4 or **5** use this finger

1 = thumb 2 = index finger 3 = middle finger 4 = ring finger 5 = little finger

Chord Spelling

1st (F#), 3rd (A#), #5th (Cx)

F#sus4
F# Suspended 4th

Middle C

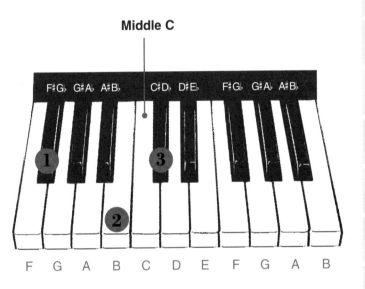

use this note

1 2 3 4 or **5** use this finger

1 = thumb 2 = index finger 3 = middle finger 4 = ring finger 5 = little finger

Chord Spelling

1st (F#), 4th (B), 5th (C#)

F♯o/F♯dim
F♯ Diminished Triad

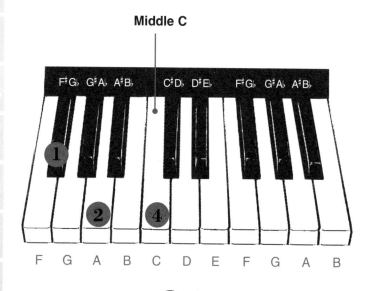

Middle C

F♯G♭ G♯A♭ A♯B♭   C♯D♭ D♯E♭   F♯G♭ G♯A♭ A♯B♭

F G A B C D E F G A B

● use this note

1 2 3 4 or **5**   use this finger

1 = thumb   2 = index finger   3 = middle finger   4 = ring finger   5 = little finger

Chord Spelling

1st (F♯), ♭3rd (A), ♭5th (C)

F#6
F# Major 6th

Middle C

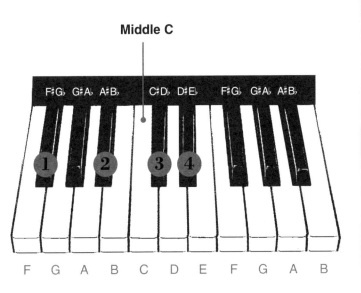

F G A B C D E F G A B

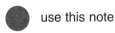 use this note

1 2 3 4 or **5** use this finger

1 = thumb 2 = index finger 3 = middle finger 4 = ring finger 5 = little finger

Chord Spelling

1st (F#), 3rd (A#), 5th (C#), 6th (D#)

F#m6
F# Minor 6th

Middle C

use this note

1 2 3 4 or **5** use this finger

1 = thumb 2 = index finger 3 = middle finger 4 = ring finger 5 = little finger

Chord Spelling

1st (F#), ♭3rd (A), 5th (C#), 6th (D#)

F#maj7
F# Major 7th

Middle C

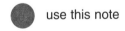

F#G♭ G#A♭ A#B♭   C#D♭ D#E♭   F#G♭ G#A♭ A#B♭

F G A B C D E F G A B

use this note

1 2 3 4 or **5** use this finger

1 = thumb **2** = index finger **3** = middle finger **4** = ring finger **5** = little finger

F#/G♭

Chord Spelling

1st (F#), 3rd (A#), 5th (C#), 7th (F)

F#m7
F# Minor 7th

Middle C

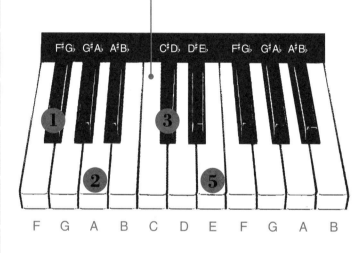

F#G♭ G#A♭ A#B♭   C#D♭ D#E♭   F#G♭ G#A♭ A#B♭

F   G   A   B   C   D   E   F   G   A   B

● use this note

1 2 3 4 or **5** use this finger

1 = thumb   2 = index finger   3 = middle finger   4 = ring finger   5 = little finger

Chord Spelling

1st (F#), ♭3rd (A), 5th (C#), ♭7th (E)

F#7
F# Dominant 7th

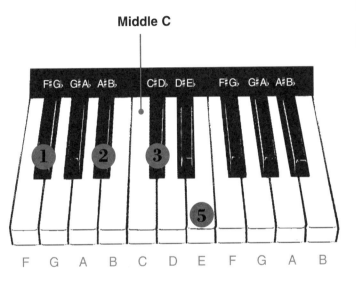

Middle C

F#G♭ G#A♭ A#B♭   C#D♭ D#E♭   F#G♭ G#A♭ A#B♭

F   G   A   B   C   D   E   F   G   A   B

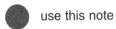 use this note

1 2 3 4 or **5** use this finger

1 = thumb   2 = index finger   3 = middle finger   4 = ring finger   5 = little finger

Chord Spelling

1st (F#), 3rd (A#), 5th (C#), ♭7th (E)

F#7sus4
F# Dominant 7th sus4

Middle C

F#G♭ G#A♭ A#B♭   C#D♭ D#E♭   F#G♭ G#A♭ A#B♭

F G A B C D E F G A B

● use this note

1 2 3 4 or **5** use this finger

1 = thumb 2 = index finger 3 = middle finger 4 = ring finger 5 = little finger

Chord Spelling

1st (F#), 4th (B), 5th (C#), ♭7th (E)

F♯7+5
F♯ Dominant 7th
Augmented 5th

Middle C

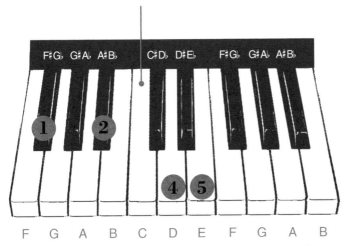

use this note

1 2 3 4 or **5** use this finger

1 = thumb 2 = index finger 3 = middle finger 4 = ring finger 5 = little finger

Chord Spelling

1st (F♯), 3rd (A♯), ♯5th (Cx), ♭7th (E)

F#7-5
F# Dominant 7th
Flattened 5th

Middle C

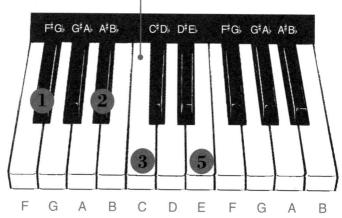

use this note

1 2 3 4 or **5** use this finger

1 = thumb   2 = index finger   3 = middle finger   4 = ring finger   5 = little finger

Chord Spelling

1st (F#), 3rd (A#), b5th (C), b7th (E)

F#dim7
F# Diminished 7th

Middle C

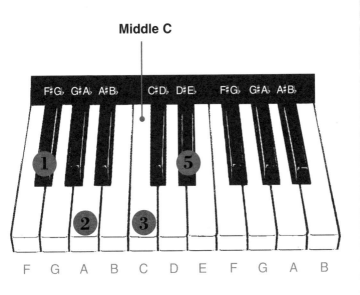

F#G♭ G#A♭ A#B♭   C#D♭ D#E♭   F#G♭ G#A♭ A#B♭

F G A B C D E F G A B

use this note

1 2 3 4 or **5** use this finger

1 = thumb   2 = index finger   3 = middle finger   4 = ring finger   5 = little finger

F#/G♭

Chord Spelling

1st (F#), ♭3rd (A), ♭5th (C), ♭♭7th (E♭)

F♯m7-5
F♯ Minor 7th
Flattened 5th

Middle C

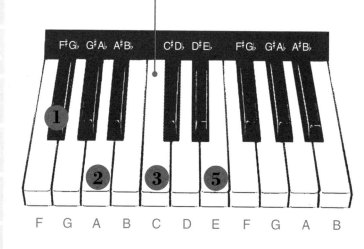

use this note

1 2 3 4 or **5** use this finger

1 = thumb   2 = index finger   3 = middle finger   4 = ring finger   5 = little finger

Chord Spelling

1st (F♯), ♭3rd (A), ♭5th (C), ♭7th (E)

F#mmaj7
F# Minor-Major 7th

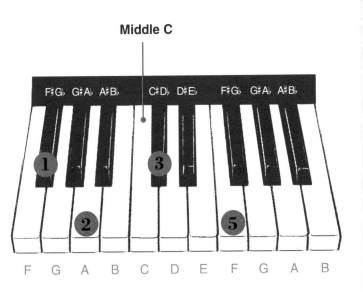

Middle C

F#G♭ G#A♭ A#B♭   C#D♭ D#E♭   F#G♭ G#A♭ A#B♭

F G A B C D E F G A B

● use this note

1 2 3 4 or **5** use this finger

1 = thumb 2 = index finger 3 = middle finger 4 = ring finger 5 = little finger

F#/G♭

Chord Spelling

1st (F#), ♭3rd (A), 5th (C#), 7th (E#)

F#maj9
F# Major 9th

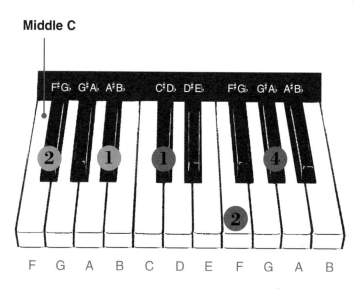

Middle C

F#G♭ G#A♭ A#B♭ C#D♭ D#E♭ F#G♭ G#A♭ A#B♭

F G A B C D E F G A B

use this note

1 2 3 4 or **5** use this finger

1 = thumb 2 = index finger 3 = middle finger 4 = ring finger 5 = little finger

Chord Spelling

1st (F#), 3rd (A#), 5th (C#), 7th (E#), 9th (G#)

F#m9
F# Minor 9th

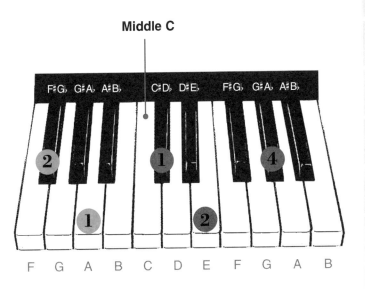

Middle C

 use this note

1 2 3 4 or **5** use this finger

1 = thumb   2 = index finger   3 = middle finger   4 = ring finger   5 = little finger

Chord Spelling

1st (F#), ♭3rd (A), 5th (C#), ♭7th (E), 9th (G#)

F#9
F# Dominant 9th

Middle C

F#G♭ G#A♭ A#B♭   C#D♭ D#E♭   F#G♭ G#A♭ A#B♭

F G A B C D E F G A B

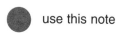 use this note

1 2 3 4 or **5** use this finger

1 = thumb   2 = index finger   3 = middle finger   4 = ring finger   5 = little finger

Chord Spelling

1st (F#), 3rd (A#), 5th (C#), ♭7th (E), 9th (G#)

F♯9+5
F♯ 9th Augmented 5th

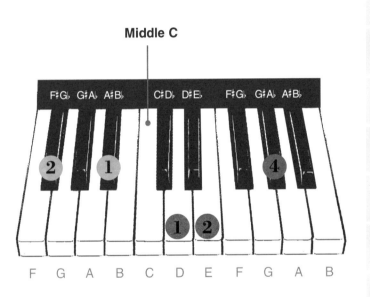

Middle C

F♯G♭ G♯A♭ A♯B♭   C♯D♭ D♯E♭   F♯G♭ G♯A♭ A♯B♭

F G A B C D E F G A B

use this note

1 2 3 4 or **5** use this finger

1 = thumb 2 = index finger 3 = middle finger 4 = ring finger 5 = little finger

F♯/G♭

Chord Spelling

1st (F♯), 3rd (A♯), ♯5th (Cx), ♭7th (E), 9th (G♯)

F♯9-5
F♯ 9th Flattened 5th

Middle C

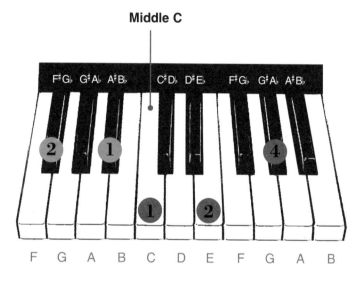

use this note

1 2 3 4 or **5** use this finger

1 = thumb 2 = index finger 3 = middle finger 4 = ring finger 5 = little finger

Chord Spelling

1st (F♯), 3rd (A♯), ♭5th (C), ♭7th (E), 9th (G♯)

F♯9/6
F♯ 9th Add 6th

Middle C

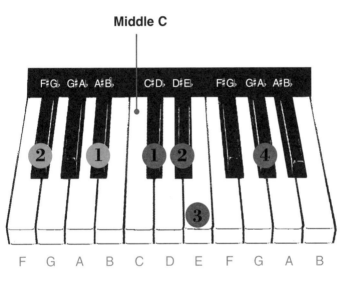

🔵 use this note

1 2 3 4 or **5** use this finger

1 = thumb   2 = index finger   3 = middle finger   4 = ring finger   5 = little finger

Chord Spelling

1st (F♯), 3rd (A♯), 5th (C♯), 6th (D♯), ♭7th (E), 9th (G♯)

F#maj11
F# Major 11th

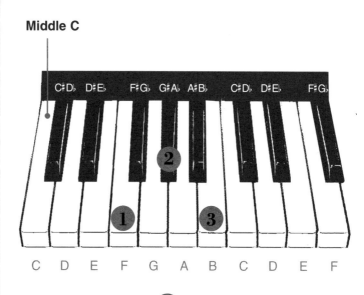

Middle C

use this note

1 2 3 4 or **5** use this finger

1 = thumb 2 = index finger 3 = middle finger 4 = ring finger 5 = little finger

Chord Spelling

1st (F#), 3rd (A#), 5th (C#), 7th (E#), 9th (G#), 11th (B)

F#m11
F# Minor 11th

Middle C

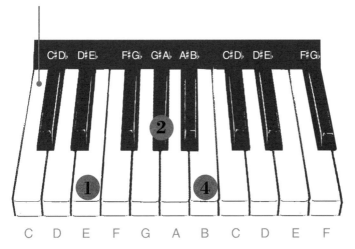

use this note

1 2 3 4 or **5** use this finger

1 = thumb 2 = index finger 3 = middle finger 4 = ring finger 5 = little finger

F#/G♭

Chord Spelling

1st (F#), ♭3rd (A), 5th (C#), ♭7th (E), 9th (G#), 11th (B)

F#11
F# Dominant 11th

Middle C

C♯D♭ D♯E♭ F♯G♭ G♯A♭ A♯B♭ C♯D♭ D♯E♭ F♯G♭

C D E F G A B C D E F

● use this note

1 2 3 4 or 5 use this finger

1 = thumb 2 = index finger 3 = middle finger 4 = ring finger 5 = little finger

Chord Spelling

1st (F#), 3rd (A#), 5th (C#), ♭7th (E), 9th (G#), 11th (B)

F#11-9
F# 11th Flattened 9th

Middle C

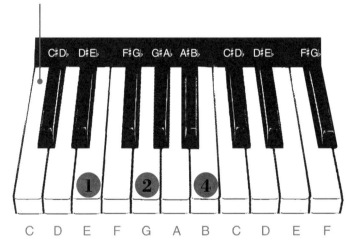

use this note

1 2 3 4 or **5** use this finger

1 = thumb 2 = index finger 3 = middle finger 4 = ring finger 5 = little finger

Chord Spelling

1st (F#), 3rd (A#), 5th (C#), ♭7th (E), ♭9th (G), 11th (B)

F#maj13
F# Major 13th

Middle C

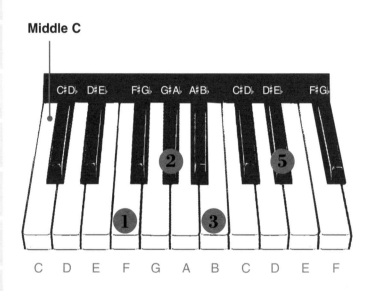

use this note

1 2 3 4 or **5** use this finger

1 = thumb 2 = index finger 3 = middle finger 4 = ring finger 5 = little finger

Chord Spelling

1st (F#), 3rd (A#), 5th (C#), 7th (E#), 9th (G#), 11th (B), 13th (D#)

F#m13
F# Minor 13th

Middle C

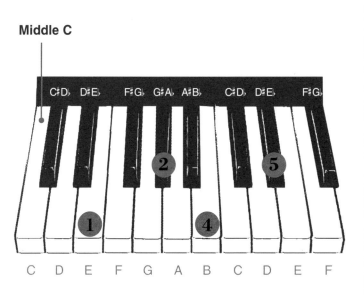

use this note

1 2 3 4 or **5** use this finger

1 = thumb 2 = index finger 3 = middle finger 4 = ring finger 5 = little finger

Chord Spelling

1st (F#), ♭3rd (A), 5th (C#), ♭7th (E), 9th (G#), 11th (B), 13th (D#)

F#13
F# Dominant 13th

Middle C

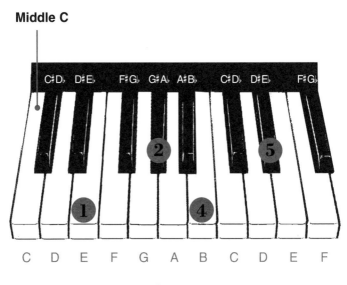

C D E F G A B C D E F

use this note

1 2 3 4 or **5** use this finger

1 = thumb 2 = index finger 3 = middle finger 4 = ring finger 5 = little finger

Chord Spelling

1st (F#), 3rd (A#), 5th (C#), ♭7th (E), 9th (G#), 11th (B), 13th (D#)

A
B♭/A#
B
C
C#/D♭
D
E♭/D#
E
F
F#/G♭
G
A♭/G#

F♯13-9
F♯ 13th Flattened 9th

Middle C

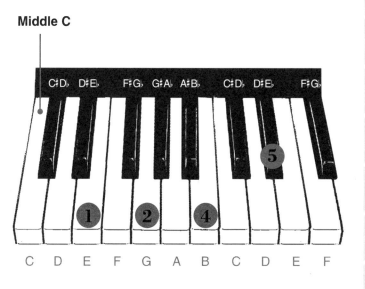

C D E F G A B C D E F

use this note

1 2 3 4 or **5** use this finger

1 = thumb 2 = index finger 3 = middle finger 4 = ring finger 5 = little finger

Chord Spelling

st (F♯), 3rd (A♯), 5th (C♯), ♭7th (E), ♭9th (G), 11th (B), 13th (D♯)

G
G Major

Middle C

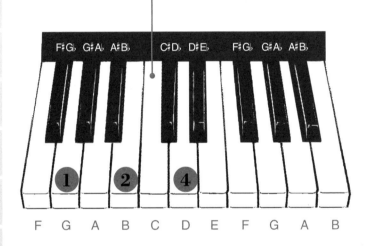

F G A B C D E F G A B

use this note

1 2 3 4 or **5** use this finger

1 = thumb 2 = index finger 3 = middle finger 4 = ring finger 5 = little finger

Chord Spelling

1st (G), 3rd (B), 5th (D)

Gm
G Minor

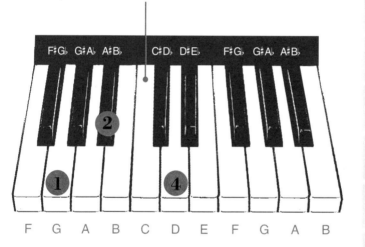

Middle C

F#G♭ G#A♭ A#B♭ | C#D♭ D#E♭ | F#G♭ G#A♭ A#B♭

F G A B C D E F G A B

use this note

1 2 3 4 or **5** use this finger

1 = thumb 2 = index finger 3 = middle finger 4 = ring finger 5 = little finger

Chord Spelling

1st (G), ♭3rd (B♭), 5th (D)

G+/Gaug
G Augmented Triad

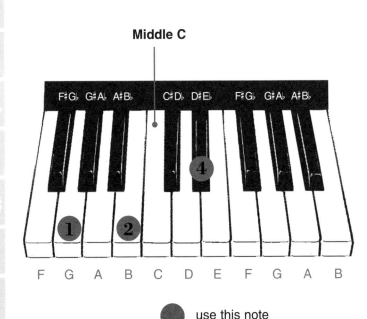

Middle C

F♯G♭ G♯A♭ A♯B♭   C♯D♭ D♯E♭   F♯G♭ G♯A♭ A♯B♭

F G A B C D E F G A B

use this note

1 2 3 4 or **5** use this finger

1 = thumb **2** = index finger **3** = middle finger **4** = ring finger **5** = little finger

A
B♭/A♯
B
C
C♯/D♭
D
E♭/D♯
E
F
F♯/G♭
G
A♭/G♯

Chord Spelling

1st (G), 3rd (B), ♯5th (D♯)

Gsus4
G Suspended 4th

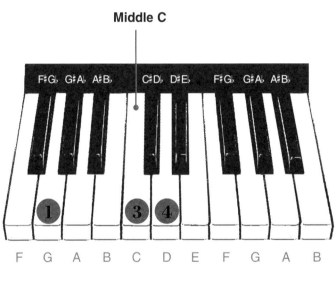

Middle C

F#G♭ G#A♭ A#B♭   C#D♭ D#E♭   F#G♭ G#A♭ A#B♭

F G A B C D E F G A B

use this note

1 2 3 4 or **5** use this finger

1 = thumb 2 = index finger 3 = middle finger 4 = ring finger 5 = little finger

Chord Spelling

1st (G), 4th (C), 5th (D)

Go/Gdim
G Diminished Triad

Middle C

F G A B C D E F G A B

● use this note

1 2 3 4 or **5** use this finger

1 = thumb 2 = index finger 3 = middle finger 4 = ring finger 5 = little finger

Chord Spelling

1st (G), ♭3rd (B♭), ♭5th (D♭)

G6
G Major 6th

Middle C

F G A B C D E F G A B

use this note

1 2 3 4 or **5** use this finger

1 = thumb 2 = index finger 3 = middle finger 4 = ring finger 5 = little finger

Chord Spelling

1st (G), 3rd (B), 5th (D), 6th (E)

Gm6
G Minor 6th

Middle C

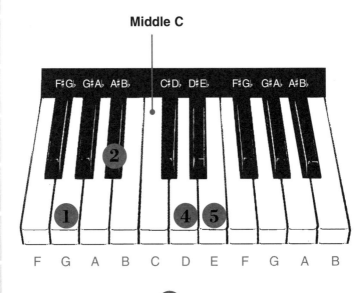

F G A B C D E F G A B

use this note

1 2 3 4 or **5** use this finger

1 = thumb 2 = index finger 3 = middle finger 4 = ring finger 5 = little finger

Chord Spelling

1st (G), ♭3rd (B♭), 5th (D), 6th (E)

Gmaj7
G Major 7th

Middle C

F#G♭ G#A♭ A#B♭ C#D♭ D#E♭ F#G♭ G#A♭ A#B♭

5

1 **2** **4**

F G A B C D E F G A B

use this note

1 2 3 4 or **5** use this finger

1 = thumb **2** = index finger **3** = middle finger **4** = ring finger **5** = little finger

G

Chord Spelling

1st (G), 3rd (B), 5th (D), 7th (F#)

Gm7
G Minor 7th

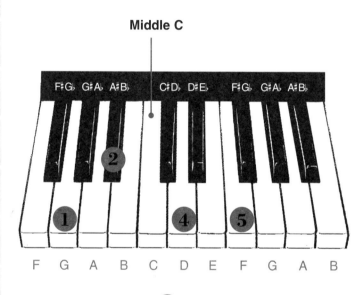

Middle C

F#G♭ G#A♭ A#B♭   C#D♭ D#E♭   F#G♭ G#A♭ A#B♭

F G A B C D E F G A B

use this note

1 2 3 4 or **5**   use this finger

1 = thumb   **2** = index finger   **3** = middle finger   **4** = ring finger   **5** = little finger

Chord Spelling

1st (G), ♭3rd (B♭), 5th (D), ♭7th (F)

G7
G Dominant 7th

Middle C

F G A B C D E F G A B

use this note

1 2 3 4 or **5** use this finger

1 = thumb   2 = index finger   3 = middle finger   4 = ring finger   5 = little finger

Chord Spelling

1st (G), 3rd (B), 5th (D), ♭7th (F)

G7sus4
G Dominant 7th sus4

Middle C

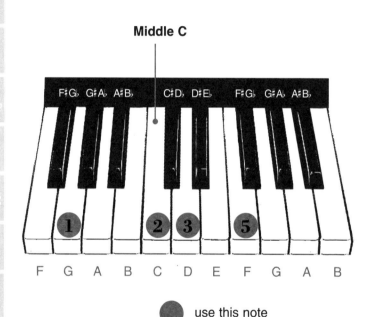

F G A B C D E F G A B

🔴 use this note

1 2 3 4 or **5** use this finger

1 = thumb 2 = index finger 3 = middle finger 4 = ring finger 5 = little finger

Chord Spelling

1st (G), 4th (C), 5th (D), ♭7th (F)

G7+5
G Dominant 7th
Augmented 5th

Middle C

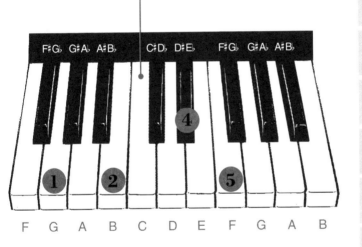

F G A B C D E F G A B

use this note

1 2 3 4 or **5** use this finger

1 = thumb   2 = index finger   3 = middle finger   4 = ring finger   5 = little finger

Chord Spelling

1st (G), 3rd (B), #5th (D#), ♭7th (F)

A
B♭/A#
B
C
C#/D♭
D
E♭/D#
E
F
F#/G♭
G
A♭/G#

G7-5
G Dominant 7th
Flattened 5th

Middle C

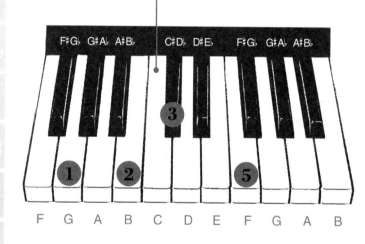

use this note

1 2 3 4 or **5** use this finger

1 = thumb   2 = index finger   3 = middle finger   4 = ring finger   5 = little finger

Chord Spelling

1st (G), 3rd (B), ♭5th (D♭), ♭7th (F)

Gdim7
G Diminished 7th

Middle C

F G A B C D E F G A B

use this note

1 2 3 4 or **5** use this finger

1 = thumb 2 = index finger 3 = middle finger 4 = ring finger 5 = little finger

G

Chord Spelling

1st (G), ♭3rd (B♭), ♭5th (D♭), ♭♭7th (F♭)

Gm7-5
G Minor 7th
Flattened 5th

Middle C

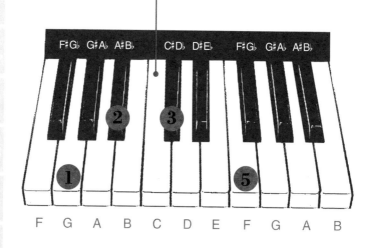

F G A B C D E F G A B

use this note

1 2 3 4 or **5** use this finger

1 = thumb 2 = index finger 3 = middle finger 4 = ring finger 5 = little finger

Chord Spelling

1st (G), ♭3rd (B♭), ♭5th (D♭), ♭7th (F)

Gmmaj7
G Minor-Major 7th

Middle C

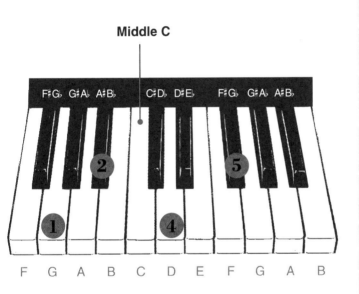

use this note

1 2 3 4 or **5** use this finger

1 = thumb   2 = index finger   3 = middle finger   4 = ring finger   5 = little finger

Chord Spelling

1st (G), ♭3rd (B♭), 5th (D), 7th (F♯)

Gmaj9
G Major 9th

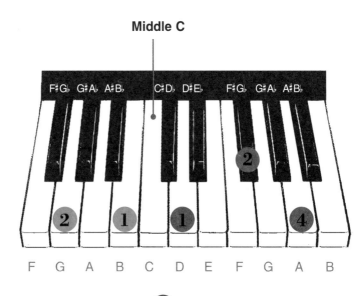

Middle C

F G A B C D E F G A B

use this note

1 2 3 4 or **5** use this finger

1 = thumb 2 = index finger 3 = middle finger 4 = ring finger 5 = little finger

Chord Spelling

1st (G), 3rd (B), 5th (D), 7th (F#), 9th (A)

Gm9
G Minor 9th

Middle C

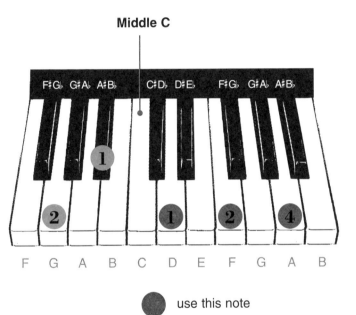

use this note

1 2 3 4 or **5** use this finger

1 = thumb **2 =** index finger **3 =** middle finger **4 =** ring finger **5 =** little finger

Chord Spelling

1st (G), ♭3rd (B♭), 5th (D), ♭7th (F), 9th (A)

G9
G Dominant 9th

Middle C

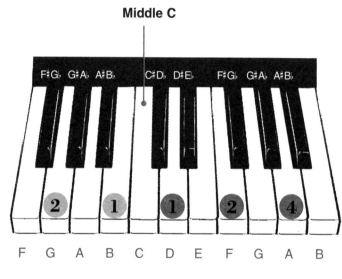

use this note

1 2 3 4 or **5**   use this finger

1 = thumb   **2** = index finger   **3** = middle finger   **4** = ring finger   **5** = little finger

Chord Spelling

1st (G), 3rd (B), 5th (D), ♭7th (F), 9th (A)

G9+5
G 9th Augmented 5th

Middle C

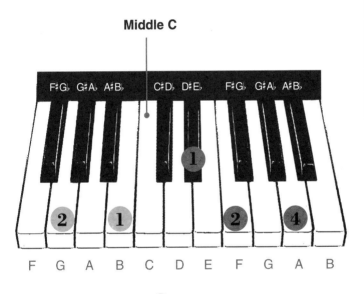

use this note

1 2 3 4 or **5** use this finger

1 = thumb   2 = index finger   3 = middle finger   4 = ring finger   5 = little finger

Chord Spelling

1st (G), 3rd (B), ♯5th (D♯), ♭7th (F), 9th (A)

G9-5
G 9th Flattened 5th

Middle C

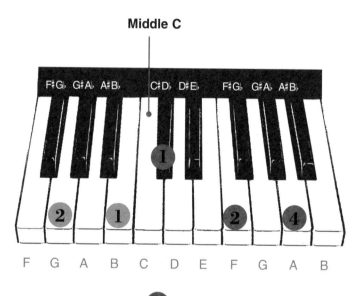

F G A B C D E F G A B

use this note

1 2 3 4 or **5** use this finger

1 = thumb 2 = index finger 3 = middle finger 4 = ring finger 5 = little finger

Chord Spelling

1st (G), 3rd (B), ♭5th (D♭), ♭7th (F), 9th (A)

G9/6
G 9th Add 6th

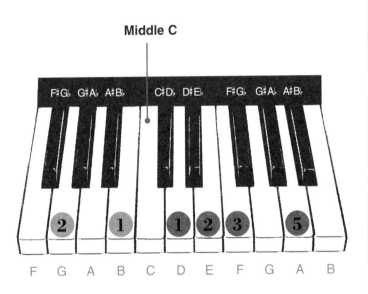

Middle C

F#G♭ G#A♭ A#B♭   C#D♭ D#E♭   F#G♭ G#A♭ A#B♭

② ① ① ② ③ ⑤

F G A B C D E F G A B

 use this note

1 2 3 4 or **5**   use this finger

1 = thumb   2 = index finger   3 = middle finger   4 = ring finger   5 = little finger

G

Chord Spelling

1st (G), 3rd (B), 5th (D), 6th (E), ♭7th (F), 9th (A)

Gmaj11
G Major 11th

Middle C

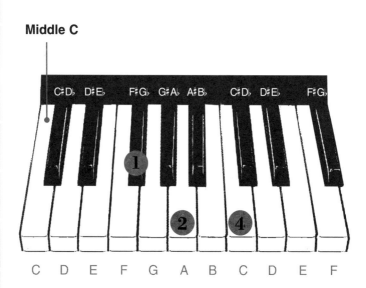

use this note

1 2 3 4 or **5** use this finger

1 = thumb 2 = index finger 3 = middle finger 4 = ring finger 5 = little finger

Chord Spelling

1st (G), 3rd (B), 5th (D), 7th (F#), 9th (A), 11th (C)

Gm11
G Minor 11th

Middle C

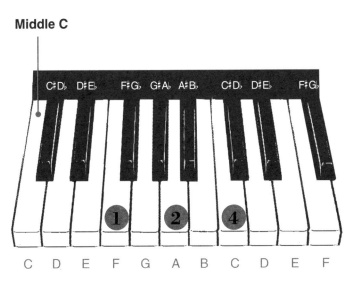

🔘 use this note

1 2 3 4 or **5** use this finger

1 = thumb 2 = index finger 3 = middle finger 4 = ring finger 5 = little finger

Chord Spelling

1st (G), ♭3rd (B♭), 5th (D), ♭7th (F), 9th (A), 11th (C)

G11
G Dominant 11th

Middle C

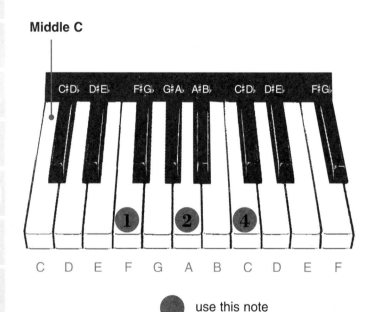

C#D♭ D#E♭ F#G♭ G#A♭ A#B♭ C#D♭ D#E♭ F#G♭

C D E F G A B C D E F

use this note

1 2 3 4 or **5** use this finger

1 = thumb 2 = index finger 3 = middle finger 4 = ring finger 5 = little finger

Chord Spelling

1st (G), 3rd (B), 5th (D), ♭7th (F), 9th (A), 11th (C)

G11-9
G 11th Flattened 9th

Middle C

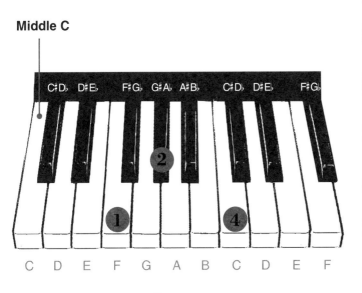

C D E F G A B C D E F

use this note

1 2 3 4 or **5** use this finger

1 = thumb 2 = index finger 3 = middle finger 4 = ring finger 5 = little finger

Chord Spelling

1st (G), 3rd (B), 5th (D), ♭7th (F), ♭9th (A♭), 11th (C)

Gmaj13
G Major 13th

Middle C

C D E F G A B C D E F

🔵 use this note

1 2 3 4 or **5** use this finger

1 = thumb 2 = index finger 3 = middle finger 4 = ring finger 5 = little finger

Chord Spelling

1st (G), 3rd (B), 5th (D), 7th (F#), 9th (A), 11th (C), 13th (E)

Gm13
G Minor 13th

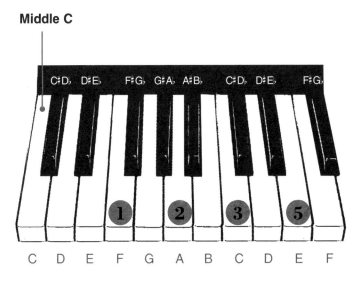

Middle C

C#D♭   D#E♭   F#G♭   G#A♭   A#B♭   C#D♭   D#E♭   F#G♭

C   D   E   F   G   A   B   C   D   E   F

use this note

1 2 3 4 or **5**   use this finger

1 = thumb   2 = index finger   3 = middle finger   4 = ring finger   5 = little finger

Chord Spelling

1st (G), ♭3rd (B♭), 5th (D), ♭7th (F), 9th (A), 11th (C), 13th (E)

4   **2**   **1**

G13
G Dominant 13th

Middle C

C#D♭ D#E♭   F#G♭ G#A♭ A#B♭   C#D♭ D#E♭   F#G♭

C D E F G A B C D E F

use this note

1 2 3 4 or **5** use this finger

1 = thumb 2 = index finger 3 = middle finger 4 = ring finger 5 = little finger

Chord Spelling

1st (G), 3rd (B), 5th (D), ♭7th (F), 9th (A), 11th (C), 13th (E)

G13-9
G 13th Flattened 9th

Middle C

C D E F G A B C D E F

use this note

1 2 3 4 or **5** use this finger

1 = thumb   2 = index finger   3 = middle finger   4 = ring finger   5 = little finger

Chord Spelling

1st (G), 3rd (B), 5th (D), ♭7th (F), ♭9th (A♭), 11th (C), 13th (E)

A♭
A♭ Major

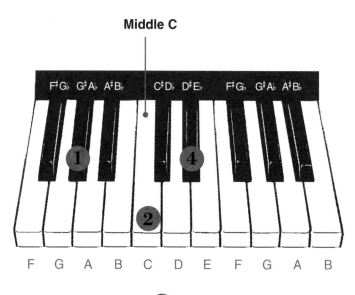

Middle C

F♯G♭ G♯A♭ A♯B♭   C♯D♭ D♯E♭   F♯G♭ G♯A♭ A♯B♭

F G A B C D E F G A B

use this note

1 2 3 4 or **5** use this finger

1 = thumb   2 = index finger   3 = middle finger   4 = ring finger   5 = little finger

Chord Spelling

1st (A♭), 3rd (C), 5th (E♭)

A♭m
A♭ Minor

Middle C

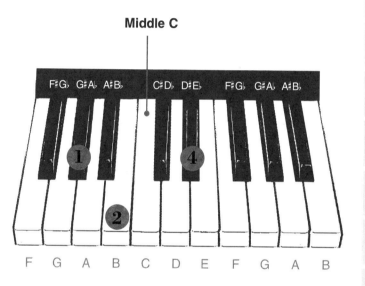

F G A B C D E F G A B

⬤ use this note

1 2 3 4 or **5** use this finger

1 = thumb   2 = index finger   3 = middle finger   4 = ring finger   5 = little finger

Chord Spelling

1st (A♭), ♭3rd (C♭), 5th (E♭)

A♭/G♯

A♭+/A♭aug
A♭ Augmented Triad

Middle C

F♯G♭ G♯A♭ A♯B♭   C♯D♭ D♯E♭   F♯G♭ G♯A♭ A♯B♭

F G A B C D E F G A B

use this note

1 2 3 4 or **5** use this finger

1 = thumb 2 = index finger 3 = middle finger 4 = ring finger 5 = little finger

Chord Spelling

1st (A♭), 3rd (C), ♯5th (E)

A B♭/A♯ B C C♯/D♭ D E♭/D♯ E F F♯/G♭ G A♭/G♯

A♭sus4
A♭ Suspended 4th

Middle C

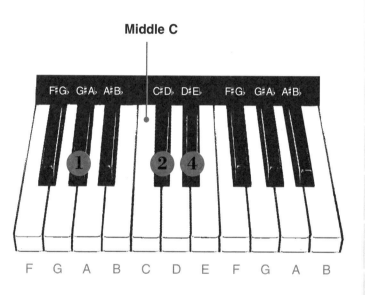

F G A B C D E F G A B

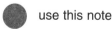 use this note

1 2 3 4 or **5** use this finger

1 = thumb 2 = index finger 3 = middle finger 4 = ring finger 5 = little finger

Chord Spelling

1st (A♭), 4th (D♭), 5th (E♭)

A♭/G#

A♭o/A♭dim
A♭ Diminished Triad

Middle C

F♯G♭ G♯A♭ A♯B♭   C♯D♭ D♯E♭   F♯G♭ G♯A♭ A♯B♭

F G A B C D E F G A B

use this note

1 2 3 4 or **5** use this finger

1 = thumb   2 = index finger   3 = middle finger   4 = ring finger   5 = little finger

Chord Spelling

1st (A♭), ♭3rd (C♭), ♭5th (E♭♭)

A♭6
A♭ Major 6th

Middle C

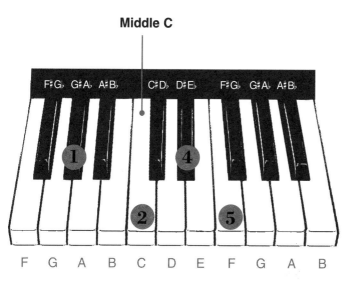

F G A B C D E F G A B

use this note

1 2 3 4 or **5** use this finger

1 = thumb 2 = index finger 3 = middle finger 4 = ring finger 5 = little finger

Chord Spelling

1st (A♭), 3rd (C), 5th (E♭), 6th (F)

A♭m6
A♭ Minor 6th

Middle C

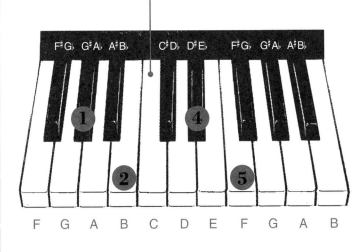

F G A B C D E F G A B

use this note

1 2 3 4 or **5** use this finger

1 = thumb 2 = index finger 3 = middle finger 4 = ring finger 5 = little finger

Chord Spelling

1st (A♭), ♭3rd (C♭), 5th (E♭), 6th (F)

A♭maj7
A♭ Major 7th

Middle C

F G A B C D E F G A B

● use this note

1 2 3 4 or **5** use this finger

1 = thumb   2 = index finger   3 = middle finger   4 = ring finger   5 = little finger

Chord Spelling

1st (A♭), 3rd (C), 5th (E♭), 7th (G)

A♭m7
A♭ Minor 7th

Middle C

F♯G♭ G♯A♭ A♯B♭   C♯D♭ D♯E♭   F♯G♭ G♯A♭ A♯B♭

F G A B C D E F G A B

 use this note

1 2 3 4 or **5** use this finger

1 = thumb 2 = index finger 3 = middle finger 4 = ring finger 5 = little finger

Chord Spelling

1st (A♭), ♭3rd (C♭), 5th (E♭), ♭7th (G♭)

A♭7
A♭ Dominant 7th

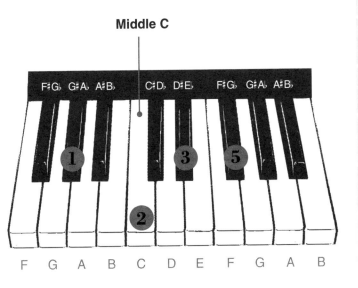

Middle C

use this note

1 2 3 4 or **5** use this finger

1 = thumb 2 = index finger 3 = middle finger 4 = ring finger 5 = little finger

Chord Spelling

1st (A♭), 3rd (C), 5th (E♭), ♭7th (G♭)

A♭/G#

A♭7sus4
A♭ Dominant 7th sus4

Middle C

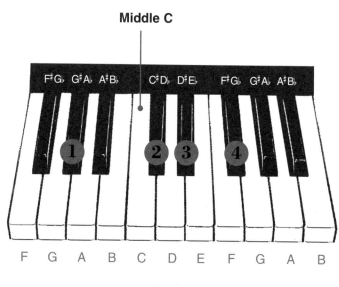

use this note

1 2 3 4 or **5** use this finger

1 = thumb **2** = index finger **3** = middle finger **4** = ring finger **5** = little finger

Chord Spelling

1st (A♭), 4th (D♭), 5th (E♭), ♭7th (G♭)

A♭7+5
A♭ Dominant 7th
Augmented 5th

Middle C

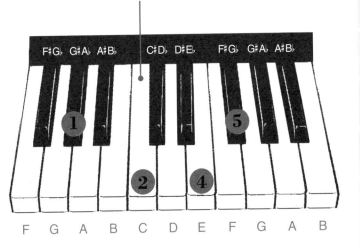

● use this note

1 2 3 4 or **5** use this finger

1 = thumb 2 = index finger 3 = middle finger 4 = ring finger 5 = little finger

Chord Spelling

1st (A♭), 3rd (C), #5th (E), ♭7th (G♭)

A♭7-5
A♭ Dominant 7th
Flattened 5th

Middle C

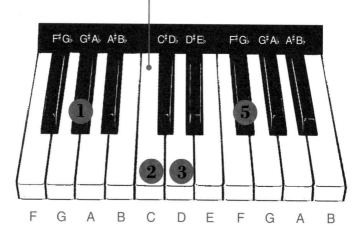

F♯G♭ G♯A♭ A♯B♭   C♯D♭ D♯E♭   F♯G♭ G♯A♭ A♯B♭

F G A B C D E F G A B

use this note

1 2 3 4 or **5**   use this finger

1 = thumb   2 = index finger   3 = middle finger   4 = ring finger   5 = little finger

Chord Spelling

1st (A♭), 3rd (C), ♭5th (E♭♭), ♭7th (G♭)

A♭dim7
A♭ Diminished 7th

Middle C

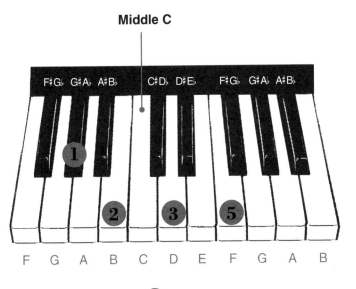

F G A B C D E F G A B

use this note

1 2 3 4 or **5** use this finger

1 = thumb   2 = index finger   3 = middle finger   4 = ring finger   5 = little finger

Chord Spelling

1st (A♭), ♭3rd (C♭), ♭5th (E♭♭), ♭♭7th (G♭♭)

A
B♭/A#
B
C
C#/D♭
D
E♭/D#
E
F
F#/G♭
G
A♭/G#

A♭m7-5
A♭ Minor 7th
Flattened 5th

Middle C

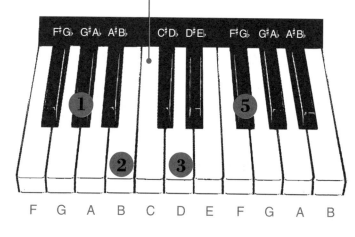

use this note

1 2 3 4 or **5** use this finger

1 = thumb 2 = index finger 3 = middle finger 4 = ring finger 5 = little finger

Chord Spelling

1st (A♭), ♭3rd (C♭), ♭5th (E♭♭), ♭7th (G♭)

A♭mmaj7
A♭ Minor-Major 7th

Middle C

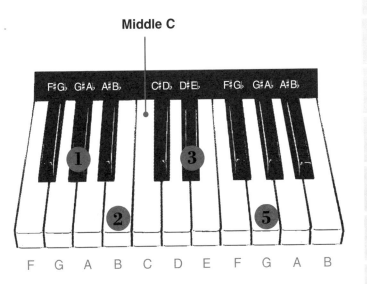

F G A B C D E F G A B

● use this note

1 2 3 4 or **5** use this finger

1 = thumb   2 = index finger   3 = middle finger   4 = ring finger   5 = little finger

Chord Spelling

1st (A♭), ♭3rd (C♭), 5th (E♭), 7th (G)

A
B♭/A♯
B
C
C♯/D♭
D
E♭/D♯
E
F
F♯/G♭
G
A♭/G♯

A♭maj9
A♭ Major 9th

Middle C

F♯G♭ G♯A♭ A♯B♭   C♯D♭ D♯E♭   F♯G♭ G♯A♭ A♯B♭

F G A B C D E F G A B

use this note

1 2 3 4 or **5** use this finger

1 = thumb   2 = index finger   3 = middle finger   4 = ring finger   5 = little finger

Chord Spelling

1st (A♭), 3rd (C), 5th (E♭), 7th (G), 9th (B♭)

A♭m9
A♭ Minor 9th

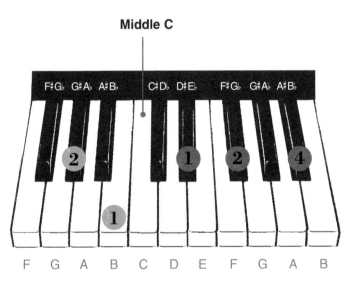

Middle C

use this note

1 2 3 4 or **5** use this finger

1 = thumb   2 = index finger   3 = middle finger   4 = ring finger   5 = little finger

Chord Spelling

1st (A♭), ♭3rd (C♭), 5th (E♭), ♭7th (G♭), 9th (B♭)

A
B♭/A♯
B
C
C♯/D♭
D
E♭/D♯
E
F
F♯/G♭
G
A♭/G♯

A♭9
A♭ Dominant 9th

Middle C

F G A B C D E F G A B

use this note

1 2 3 4 or **5** use this finger

1 = thumb **2** = index finger **3** = middle finger **4** = ring finger **5** = little finger

Chord Spelling

1st (A♭), 3rd (C), 5th (E♭), ♭7th (G♭), 9th (B♭)

A♭9+5
A♭ 9th Augmented 5th

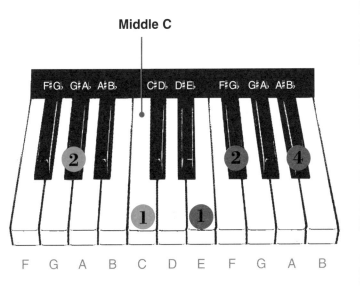

Middle C

F#G♭ G#A♭ A#B♭   C#D♭ D#E♭   F#G♭ G#A♭ A#B♭

F G A B C D E F G A B

use this note

1 2 3 4 or **5** use this finger

1 = thumb 2 = index finger 3 = middle finger 4 = ring finger 5 = little finger

Chord Spelling

1st (A♭), 3rd (C), #5th (E), ♭7th (G♭), 9th (B♭)

A♭9-5
A♭ 9th Flattened 5th

Middle C

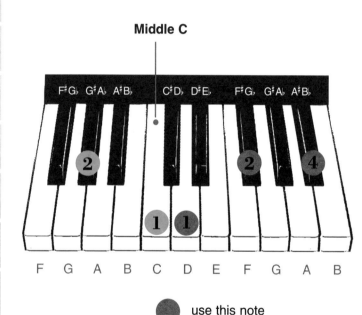

use this note

1 2 3 4 or **5** use this finger

1 = thumb 2 = index finger 3 = middle finger 4 = ring finger 5 = little finger

Chord Spelling

1st (A♭), 3rd (C), ♭5th (E♭♭), ♭7th (G♭), 9th (B♭)

A♭9/6
A♭ 9th Add 6th

A
B♭/A♯
B
C
C♯/D♭
D
E♭/D♯
E
F
F♯/G♭
G
A♭/G♯

Middle C

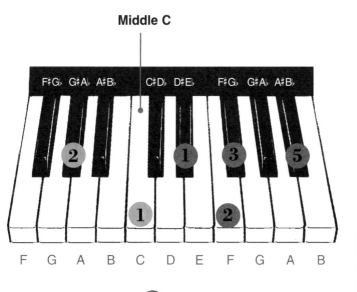

F♯G♭ G♯A♭ A♯B♭   C♯D♭ D♯E♭   F♯G♭ G♯A♭ A♯B♭

F G A B C D E F G A B

use this note

1 2 3 4 or **5** use this finger

1 = thumb 2 = index finger 3 = middle finger 4 = ring finger 5 = little finger

Chord Spelling

1st (A♭), 3rd (C), 5th (E♭), 6th (F), ♭7th (G♭), 9th (B♭)

A♭maj11
A♭ Major 11th

Middle C

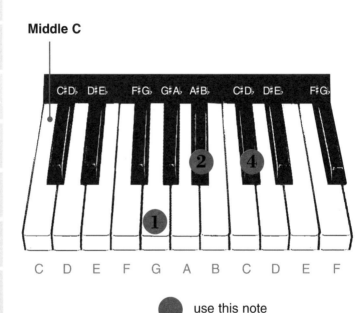

use this note

1 2 3 4 or **5** use this finger

1 = thumb 2 = index finger 3 = middle finger 4 = ring finger 5 = little finger

Chord Spelling

1st (A♭), 3rd (C), 5th (E♭), 7th (G), 9th (B♭), 11th (D♭)

A♭m11
A♭ Minor 11th

Middle C

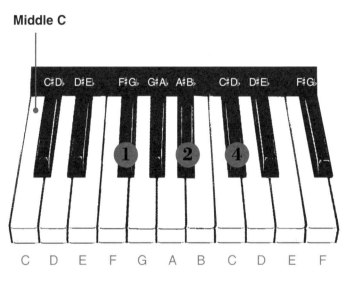

C♯D♭ D♯E♭   F♯G♭ G♯A♭ A♯B♭   C♯D♭ D♯E♭   F♯G♭

C   D   E   F   G   A   B   C   D   E   F

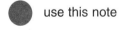 use this note

1 2 3 4 or **5** use this finger

1 = thumb 2 = index finger 3 = middle finger 4 = ring finger 5 = little finger

Chord Spelling

1st (A♭), ♭3rd (C♭), 5th (E♭), ♭7th (G♭), 9th (B♭), 11th (D♭)

A♭/G#

A♭11
A♭ Dominant 11th

Middle C

C♯D♭ D♯E♭ F♯G♭ G♯A♭ A♯B♭ C♯D♭ D♯E♭ F♯G♭

C D E F G A B C D E F

⬤ use this note

1 2 3 4 or **5** use this finger

1 = thumb 2 = index finger 3 = middle finger 4 = ring finger 5 = little finger

Chord Spelling

1st (A♭), 3rd (C), 5th (E♭), ♭7th (G♭), 9th (B♭), 11th (D♭)

A♭11-9
A♭ 11th Flattened 9th

Middle C

C D E F G A B C D E F

use this note

1 2 3 4 or **5** use this finger

1 = thumb   2 = index finger   3 = middle finger   4 = ring finger   5 = little finger

Chord Spelling

1st (A♭), 3rd (C), 5th (E♭), ♭7th (G♭), ♭9th (B♭♭), 11th (D♭)

A
B♭/A♯
B
C
C♯/D♭
D
E♭/D♯
E
F
F♯/G♭
G
A♭/G♯

A♭maj13
A♭ Major 13th

Middle C

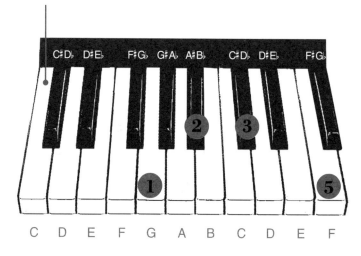

C D E F G A B C D E F

use this note

1 2 3 4 or **5** use this finger

1 = thumb 2 = index finger 3 = middle finger 4 = ring finger 5 = little finger

Chord Spelling

1st (A♭), 3rd (C), 5th (E♭), 7th (G), 9th (B♭), 11th (D♭), 13th (F)

A♭m13
A♭ Minor 13th

Middle C

C D E F G A B C D E F

use this note

1 2 3 4 or **5** use this finger

1 = thumb 2 = index finger 3 = middle finger 4 = ring finger 5 = little finger

Chord Spelling

1st (A♭), ♭3rd (C♭), 5th (E♭), ♭7th (G♭), 9th (B♭), 11th (D♭), 13th (F)

A
B♭/A#
B
C
C#/D♭
D
E♭/D#
E
F
F#/G♭
G
A♭/G#

A♭13
A♭ Dominant 13th

Middle C

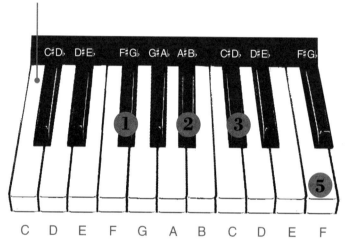

C D E F G A B C D E F

 use this note

1 2 3 4 or **5** use this finger

1 = thumb   2 = index finger   3 = middle finger   4 = ring finger   5 = little finger

Chord Spelling

1st (A♭), 3rd (C), 5th (E♭), ♭7th (G♭), 9th (B♭), 11th (D♭), 13th (F

A♭13-9
A♭ 13th Flattened 9th

Middle C

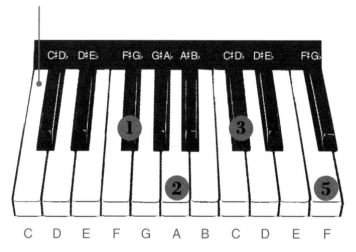

C D E F G A B C D E F

● use this note

1 2 3 4 or **5** use this finger

1 = thumb   2 = index finger   3 = middle finger   4 = ring finger   5 = little finger

Chord Spelling

1st (A♭), 3rd (C), 5th (E♭), ♭7th (G♭), ♭9th (B♭♭), 11th (D♭), 13th (F)

A
A Major

Middle C

F♯G♭ G♯A♭ A♯B♭   C♯D♭ D♯E♭   F♯G♭ G♯A♭ A♯B♭

F G A B C D E F G A B

⬤ use this note

1 2 3 4 or **5** use this finger

1 = thumb 2 = index finger 3 = middle finger 4 = ring finger 5 = little finger

Chord Spelling

1st (A), 3rd (C♯), 5th (E)

Am
A Minor

Middle C

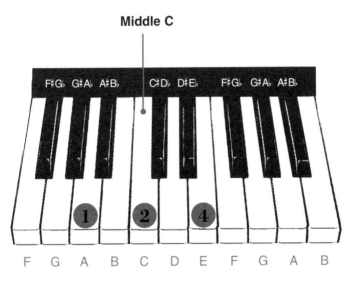

F#G♭ G#A♭ A#B♭   C#D♭ D#E♭   F#G♭ G#A♭ A#B♭

F G A B C D E F G A B

● use this note

1 2 3 4 or **5** use this finger

1 = thumb   2 = index finger   3 = middle finger   4 = ring finger   5 = little finger

Chord Spelling

1st (A), ♭3rd (C), 5th (E)

A+/Aaug
A Augmented Triad

Middle C

F♯G♭ G♯A♭ A♯B♭   C♯D♭ D♯E♭   F♯G♭ G♯A♭ A♯B♭

2

1   **4**

F G A B C D E F G A B

use this note

1 2 3 4 or **5** use this finger

1 = thumb **2** = index finger **3** = middle finger **4** = ring finger **5** = little finger

Chord Spelling

1st (A), 3rd (C♯), ♯5th (E♯)

Asus4
A Suspended 4th

Middle C

F#G♭ G#A♭ A#B♭   C#D♭ D#E♭   F#G♭ G#A♭ A#B♭

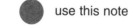

F G A B C D E F G A B

1

2 3

use this note

1 2 3 4 or **5** use this finger

1 = thumb   2 = index finger   3 = middle finger   4 = ring finger   5 = little finger

Chord Spelling

1st (A), 4th (D), 5th (E)

Ao/Adim
A Diminished Triad

Middle C

F G A B C D E F G A B

use this note

1 2 3 4 or **5** use this finger

1 = thumb   2 = index finger   3 = middle finger   4 = ring finger   5 = little finger

Chord Spelling

1st (A), ♭3rd (C), ♭5th (E♭)

A6
A Major 6th

Middle C

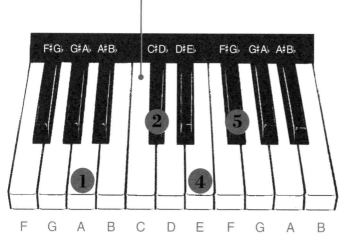

F G A B C D E F G A B

 use this note

1 2 3 4 or **5** use this finger

1 = thumb   **2** = index finger   3 = middle finger   4 = ring finger   5 = little finger

Chord Spelling

1st (A), 3rd (C♯), 5th (E), 6th (F♯)

Am6
A Minor 6th

Middle C

F♯G♭ G♯A♭ A♯B♭   C♯D♭ D♯E♭   F♯G♭ G♯A♭ A♯B♭

5

1   **2**   **4**

F G A B C D E F G A B

use this note

1 2 3 4 or **5** use this finger

1 = thumb   2 = index finger   3 = middle finger   4 = ring finger   5 = little finger

Chord Spelling

1st (A), ♭3rd (C), 5th (E), 6th (F♯)

Amaj7
A Major 7th

Middle C

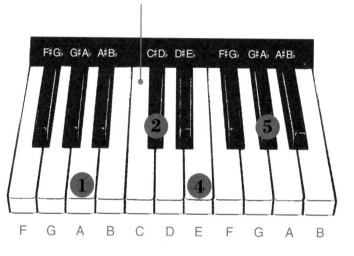

F#G♭ G#A♭ A#B♭   C#D♭ D#E♭   F#G♭ G#A♭ A#B♭

F G A B C D E F G A B

 use this note

1 2 3 4 or **5** use this finger

1 = thumb   2 = index finger   3 = middle finger   4 = ring finger   5 = little finger

Chord Spelling

1st (A), 3rd (C#), 5th (E), 7th (G#)

Am7
A Minor 7th

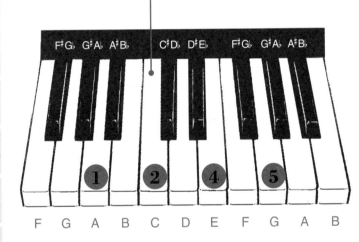

Middle C

 use this note

1 2 3 4 or **5** use this finger

1 = thumb 2 = index finger 3 = middle finger 4 = ring finger 5 = little finger

Chord Spelling

1st (A), ♭3rd (C), 5th (E), ♭7th (G)

A7
A Dominant 7th

Middle C

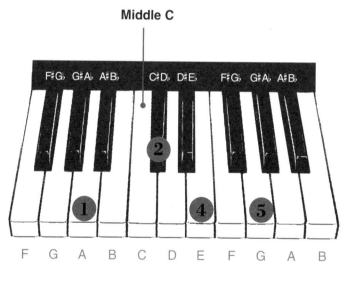

F G A B C D E F G A B

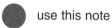 use this note

1 2 3 4 or **5** use this finger

1 = thumb   2 = index finger   3 = middle finger   4 = ring finger   5 = little finger

Chord Spelling

1st (A), 3rd (C♯), 5th (E), ♭7th (G)

A7sus4
A Dominant 7th sus4

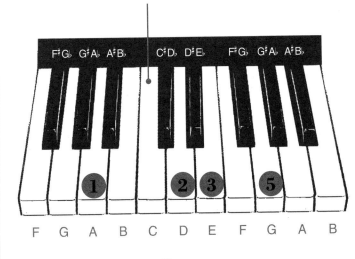

Middle C

F G A B C D E F G A B

🔴 use this note

1 2 3 4 or **5** use this finger

1 = thumb 2 = index finger 3 = middle finger 4 = ring finger 5 = little finger

Chord Spelling

1st (A), 4th (D), 5th (E), ♭7th (G)

A7+5
A Dominant 7th
Augmented 5th

Middle C

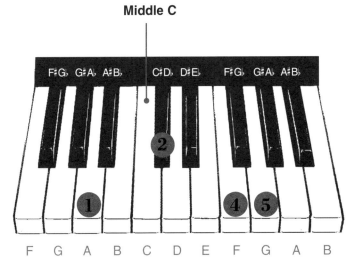

use this note

1 2 3 4 or **5** use this finger

1 = thumb 2 = index finger 3 = middle finger 4 = ring finger 5 = little finger

Chord Spelling

1st (A), 3rd (C#), #5th (E#), ♭7th (G)

A7-5
A Dominant 7th Flattened 5th

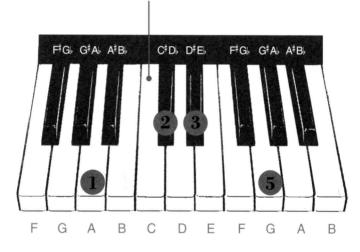

Middle C

use this note

1 2 3 4 or **5** use this finger

1 = thumb   2 = index finger   3 = middle finger   4 = ring finger   5 = little finger

Chord Spelling

1st (A), 3rd (C♯), ♭5th (E♭), ♭7th (G)

Adim7
A Diminished 7th

Middle C

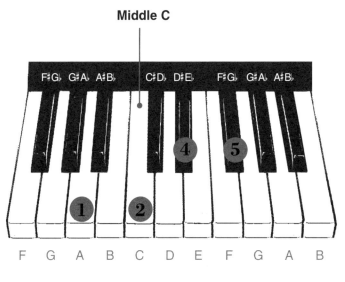

F G A B C D E F G A B

● use this note

1 2 3 4 or **5** use this finger

1 = thumb 2 = index finger 3 = middle finger 4 = ring finger 5 = little finger

Chord Spelling

1st (A), ♭3rd (C), ♭5th (E♭), ♭♭7th (G♭)

Am7-5
A Minor 7th
Flattened 5th

Middle C

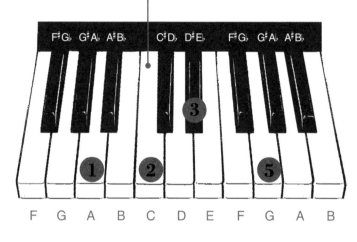

use this note

1 2 3 4 or **5** use this finger

1 = thumb 2 = index finger 3 = middle finger 4 = ring finger 5 = little finger

Chord Spelling

1st (A), ♭3rd (C), ♭5th (E♭), ♭7th (G)

Ammaj7
A Minor-Major 7th

Middle C

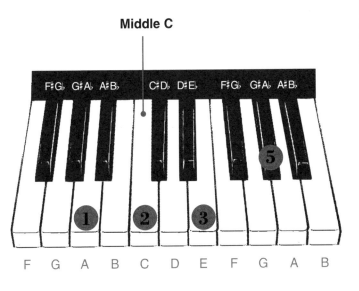

F G A B C D E F G A B

 use this note

1 2 3 4 or **5** use this finger

1 = thumb   2 = index finger   3 = middle finger   4 = ring finger   5 = little finger

Chord Spelling

1st (A), ♭3rd (C), 5th (E), 7th (G♯)

Amaj9
A Major 9th

Middle C

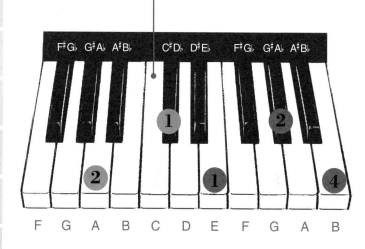

F G A B C D E F G A B

use this note

1 2 3 4 or **5** use this finger

1 = thumb   2 = index finger   3 = middle finger   4 = ring finger   5 = little finger

Chord Spelling

1st (A), 3rd (C#), 5th (E), 7th (G#), 9th (B)

Am9
A Minor 9th

Middle C

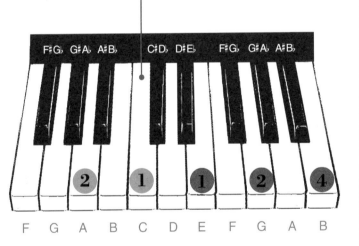

F G A B C D E F G A B

use this note

1 2 3 4 or **5** use this finger

1 = thumb 2 = index finger 3 = middle finger 4 = ring finger 5 = little finger

Chord Spelling

1st (A), ♭3rd (C), 5th (E), ♭7th (G), 9th (B)

A9
A Dominant 9th

Middle C

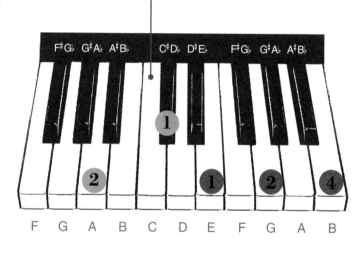

use this note

1 2 3 4 or **5** use this finger

1 = thumb   2 = index finger   3 = middle finger   4 = ring finger   5 = little finger

Chord Spelling

1st (A), 3rd (C#), 5th (E), ♭7th (G), 9th (B)

A9+5
A 9th Augmented 5th

Middle C

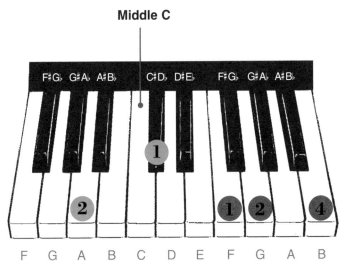

F G A B C D E F G A B

use this note

1 2 3 4 or **5** use this finger

1 = thumb   2 = index finger   3 = middle finger   4 = ring finger   5 = little finger

Chord Spelling

1st (A), 3rd (C♯), #5th (E♯), ♭7th (G), 9th (B)

A9-5
A 9th Flattened 5th

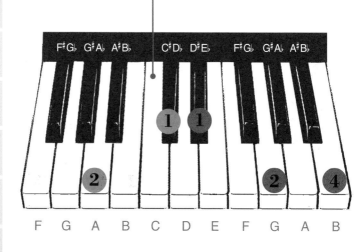

Middle C

use this note

1 2 3 4 or **5** use this finger

1 = thumb **2** = index finger **3** = middle finger **4** = ring finger **5** = little finger

Chord Spelling

1st (A), 3rd (C#), ♭5th (E♭), ♭7th (G), 9th (B)

A9/6
A 9th Add 6th

Middle C

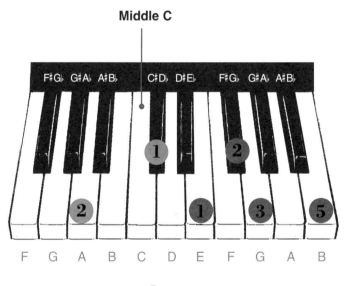

F G A B C D E F G A B

use this note

1 2 3 4 or **5** use this finger

1 = thumb   **2** = index finger   **3** = middle finger   **4** = ring finger   **5** = little finger

Chord Spelling

1st (A), 3rd (C♯), 5th (E), 6th (F♯), ♭7th (G), 9th (B)

Amaj11
A Major 11th

Middle C

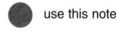

F G A B C D E F G A B

use this note

1 2 3 4 or **5** use this finger

1 = thumb 2 = index finger 3 = middle finger 4 = ring finger 5 = little finger

Chord Spelling

1st (A), 3rd (C♯), 5th (E), 7th (G♯), 9th (B), 11th (D)

Am11
A Minor 11th

Middle C

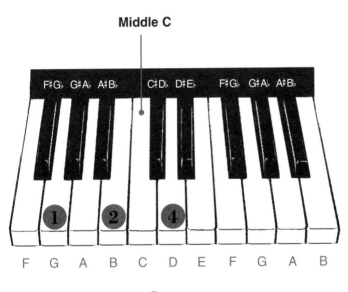

use this note

1 2 3 4 or **5** use this finger

1 = thumb　2 = index finger　3 = middle finger　4 = ring finger　5 = little finger

Chord Spelling

1st (A), ♭3rd (C), 5th (E), ♭7th (G), 9th (B), 11th (D)

A11
A Dominant 11th

Middle C

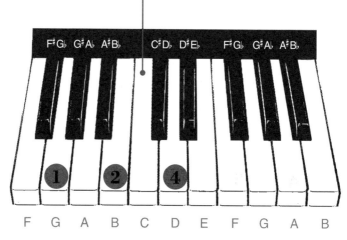

F♯G♭ G♯A♭ A♯B♭   C♯D♭ D♯E♭   F♯G♭ G♯A♭ A♯B♭

F G A B C D E F G A B

use this note

1 2 3 4 or **5** use this finger

1 = thumb   2 = index finger   3 = middle finger   4 = ring finger   5 = little finger

Chord Spelling

1st (A), 3rd (C♯), 5th (E), ♭7th (G), 9th (B), 11th (D)

A11-9
A 11th Flattened 9th

Middle C

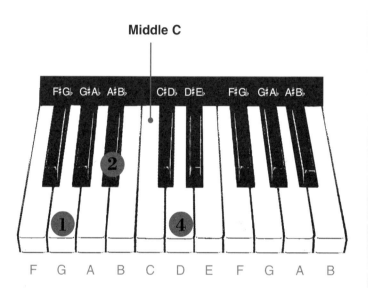

F G A B C D E F G A B

use this note

1 2 3 4 or **5** use this finger

1 = thumb 2 = index finger 3 = middle finger 4 = ring finger 5 = little finger

Chord Spelling

1st (A), 3rd (C♯), 5th (E), ♭7th (G), ♭9th (B♭), 11th (D)

4   **2**   **1**

Amaj13
A Major 13th

Middle C

F♯G♭ G♯A♭ A♯B♭   C♯D♭ D♯E♭   F♯G♭ G♯A♭ A♯B♭

F G A B C D E F G A B

1 **2** **3** **5**

⬤ use this note

1 2 3 4 or **5** use this finger

1 = thumb 2 = index finger 3 = middle finger 4 = ring finger 5 = little finger

Chord Spelling

1st (A), 3rd (C♯), 5th (E), 7th (G♯), 9th (B), 11th (D), 13th (F♯)

Am13
A Minor 13th

Middle C

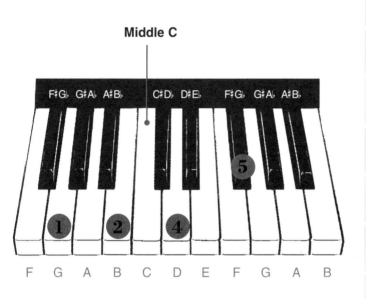

use this note

1 2 3 4 or **5** use this finger

1 = thumb 2 = index finger 3 = middle finger 4 = ring finger 5 = little finger

Chord Spelling

1st (A), ♭3rd (C), 5th (E), ♭7th (G), 9th (B), 11th (D), 13th (F♯)

A13
A Dominant 13th

Middle C

F#G♭ G#A♭ A#B♭   C#D♭ D#E♭   F#G♭ G#A♭ A#B♭

5

1   **2**   **3**

F G A B C D E F G A B

use this note

1 2 3 4 or **5** use this finger

1 = thumb 2 = index finger 3 = middle finger 4 = ring finger 5 = little finger

Chord Spelling

1st (A), 3rd (C#), 5th (E), ♭7th (G), 9th (B), 11th (D), 13th (F#)

4   **2**   **1**

A13-9
A 13th Flattened 9th

Middle C

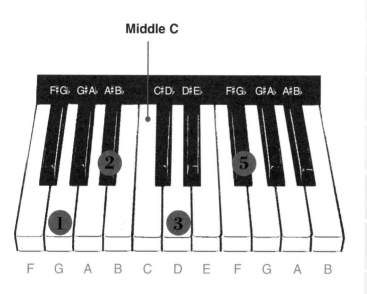

use this note

1 2 3 4 or **5** use this finger

1 = thumb 2 = index finger 3 = middle finger 4 = ring finger 5 = little finger

Chord Spelling

1st (A), 3rd (C♯), 5th (E), ♭7th (G), ♭9th (B♭), 11th (D), 13th (F♯)

B♭
B♭ Major

Middle C

F♯G♭ G♯A♭ A♯B♭   C♯D♭ D♯E♭   F♯G♭ G♯A♭ A♯B♭

F G A B C D E F G A B

● use this note

1 2 3 4 or **5** use this finger

1 = thumb 2 = index finger 3 = middle finger 4 = ring finger 5 = little finger

Chord Spelling

1st (B♭), 3rd (D), 5th (F)

B♭m
B♭ Minor

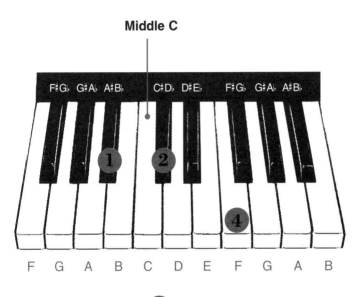

Middle C

F#G♭ G#A♭ A#B♭   C#D♭ D#E♭   F#G♭ G#A♭ A#B♭

F G A B C D E F G A B

● use this note

1 2 3 4 or **5** use this finger

1 = thumb   2 = index finger   3 = middle finger   4 = ring finger   5 = little finger

Chord Spelling

1st (B♭), ♭3rd (D♭), 5th (F)

A
B♭/A#
B
C
C#/D♭
D
E♭/D#
E
F
F#/G♭
G
A♭/G#

B♭+/B♭aug
B♭ Augmented Triad

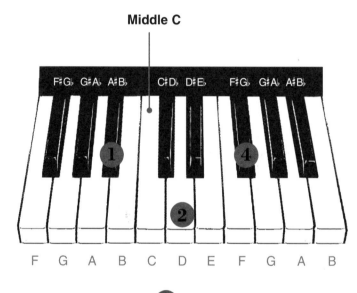

Middle C

F G A B C D E F G A B

● use this note

1 2 3 4 or **5** use this finger

1 = thumb   2 = index finger   3 = middle finger   4 = ring finger   5 = little finger

Chord Spelling

1st (B♭), 3rd (D), ♯5th (F♯)

B♭sus4
B♭ Suspended 4th

Middle C

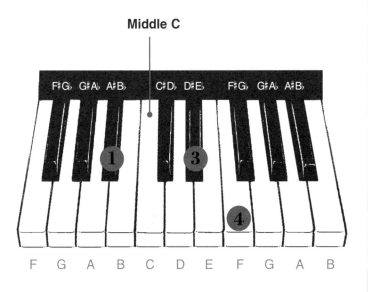

F G A B C D E F G A B

use this note

1 2 3 4 or **5** use this finger

1 = thumb   2 = index finger   3 = middle finger   4 = ring finger   5 = little finger

Chord Spelling

1st (B♭), 4th (E♭), 5th (F)

B♭o/B♭dim
B♭ Diminished Triad

Middle C

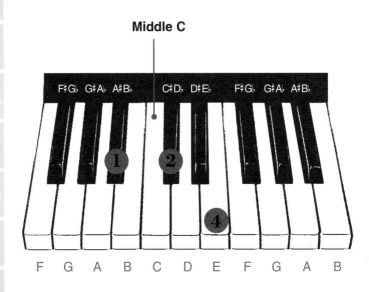

use this note

1 2 3 4 or **5** use this finger

1 = thumb   2 = index finger   3 = middle finger   4 = ring finger   5 = little finger

Chord Spelling

1st (B♭), ♭3rd (D♭), ♭5th (F♭)

B♭6
B♭ Major 6th

Middle C

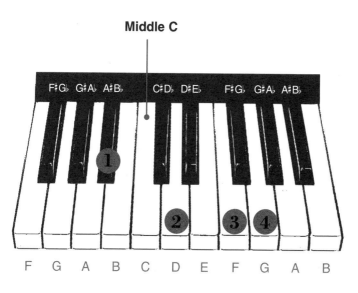

F G A B C D E F G A B

🔴 use this note

1 2 3 4 or **5** use this finger

1 = thumb   2 = index finger   3 = middle finger   4 = ring finger   5 = little finger

Chord Spelling

1st (B♭), 3rd (D), 5th (F), 6th (G)

B♭m6
B♭ Minor 6th

Middle C

F♯G♭ G♯A♭ A♯B♭   C♯D♭ D♯E♭   F♯G♭ G♯A♭ A♯B♭

F G A B C D E F G A B

use this note

1 2 3 4 or **5** use this finger

1 = thumb 2 = index finger 3 = middle finger 4 = ring finger 5 = little finger

Chord Spelling

1st (B♭), ♭3rd (D♭), 5th (F), 6th (G)

B♭maj7
B♭ Major 7th

A

B♭/A#

B

C

C#/D♭

D

E♭/D#

E

F

F#/G♭

G

A♭/G#

Middle C

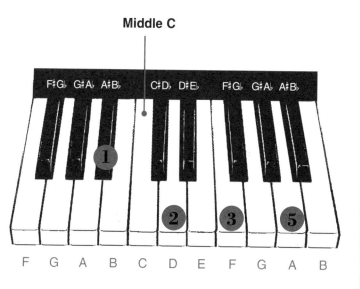

use this note

1 2 3 4 or **5** use this finger

1 = thumb 2 = index finger 3 = middle finger 4 = ring finger 5 = little finger

Chord Spelling

1st (B♭), 3rd (D), 5th (F), 7th (A)

B♭m7
B♭ Minor 7th

A
B♭/A♯
B
C
C♯/D♭
D
E♭/D♯
E
F
F♯/G♭
G
A♭/G♯

Middle C

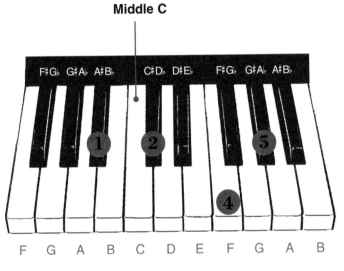

use this note

1 2 3 4 or **5** use this finger

1 = thumb   2 = index finger   3 = middle finger   4 = ring finger   5 = little finger

Chord Spelling

1st (B♭), ♭3rd (D♭), 5th (F), ♭7th (A♭)

B♭7
B♭ Dominant 7th

B♭/A♯

Middle C

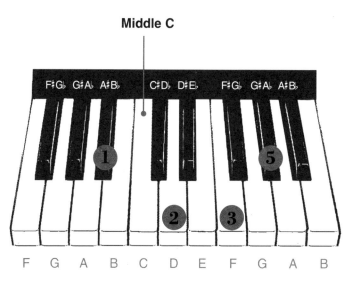

F G A B C D E F G A B

use this note

1 2 3 4 or **5** use this finger

1 = thumb   2 = index finger   3 = middle finger   4 = ring finger   5 = little finger

Chord Spelling

1st (B♭), 3rd (D), 5th (F), ♭7th (A♭)

B♭7sus4
B♭ Dominant 7th sus4

Middle C

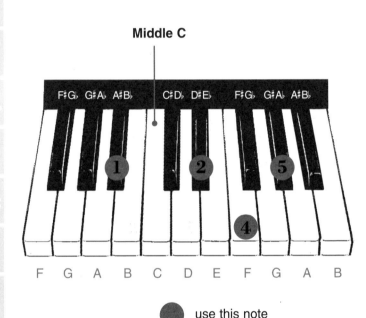

use this note

1 2 3 4 or **5** use this finger

1 = thumb   2 = index finger   3 = middle finger   4 = ring finger   5 = little finger

Chord Spelling

1st (B♭), 4th (E♭), 5th (F), ♭7th (A♭)

B♭7+5
B♭ Dominant 7th
Augmented 5th

Middle C

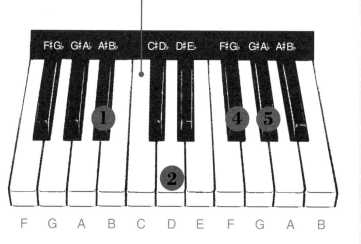

F G A B C D E F G A B

use this note

1 2 3 4 or **5** use this finger

1 = thumb 2 = index finger 3 = middle finger 4 = ring finger 5 = little finger

Chord Spelling

1st (B♭), 3rd (D), #5th (F#), ♭7th (A♭)

B♭7-5
B♭ Dominant 7th
Flattened 5th

Middle C

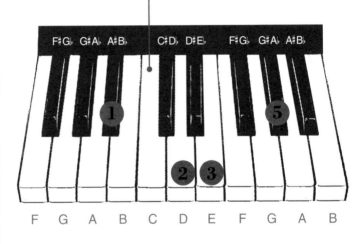

F G A B C D E F G A B

⬤ use this note

1 2 3 4 or **5** use this finger

1 = thumb 2 = index finger 3 = middle finger 4 = ring finger 5 = little finger

Chord Spelling

1st (B♭), 3rd (D), ♭5th (F♭), ♭7th (A♭)

B♭dim7
B♭ Diminished 7th

Middle C

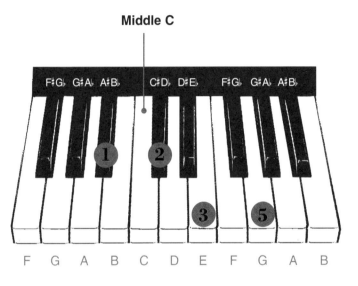

🔴 use this note

1 2 3 4 or **5** use this finger

1 = thumb 2 = index finger 3 = middle finger 4 = ring finger 5 = little finger

Chord Spelling

1st (B♭), ♭3rd (D♭), ♭5th (F♭), ♭♭7th (A♭♭)

B♭m7-5
B♭ Minor 7th
Flattened 5th

Middle C

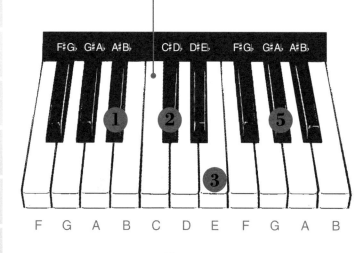

F♯G♭ G♯A♭ A♯B♭ C♯D♭ D♯E♭ F♯G♭ G♯A♭ A♯B♭

F G A B C D E F G A B

use this note

1 2 3 4 or **5** use this finger

1 = thumb 2 = index finger 3 = middle finger 4 = ring finger 5 = little finger

Chord Spelling

1st (B♭), ♭3rd (D♭), ♭5th (F♭), ♭7th (A♭)

B♭mmaj7
B♭ Minor-Major 7th

Middle C

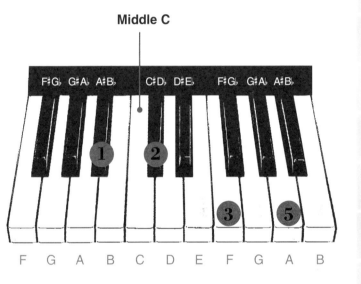

 use this note

1 2 3 4 or **5** use this finger

1 = thumb   2 = index finger   3 = middle finger   4 = ring finger   5 = little finger

Chord Spelling

1st (B♭), ♭3rd (D♭), 5th (F), 7th (A)

B♭maj9
B♭ Major 9th

Middle C

F♯G♭ G♯A♭ A♯B♭   C♯D♭ D♯E♭   F♯G♭ G♯A♭ A♯B♭

F G A B C D E F G A B

use this note

1 2 3 4 or **5** use this finger

1 = thumb 2 = index finger 3 = middle finger 4 = ring finger 5 = little finger

Chord Spelling

1st (B♭), 3rd (D), 5th (F), 7th (A), 9th (C)

B♭m9
B♭ Minor 9th

B♭/A#

Middle C

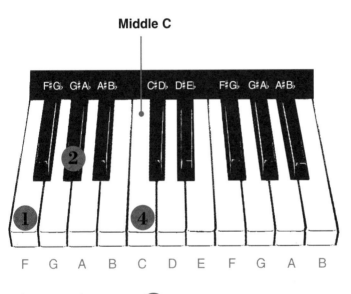

F G A B C D E F G A B

use this note

1 2 3 4 or **5** use this finger

1 = thumb 2 = index finger 3 = middle finger 4 = ring finger 5 = little finger

Chord Spelling

1st (B♭), ♭3rd (D♭), 5th (F), ♭7th (A♭), 9th (C)

B♭9
B♭ Dominant 9th

Middle C

F#G♭ G#A♭ A#B♭ C#D♭ D#E♭ F#G♭ G#A♭ A#B♭

F G A B C D E F G A B

use this note

1 2 3 4 or **5** use this finger

1 = thumb 2 = index finger 3 = middle finger 4 = ring finger 5 = little finger

Chord Spelling

1st (B♭), 3rd (D), 5th (F), ♭7th (A♭), 9th (C)

B♭9+5
B♭ 9th Augmented 5th

Middle C

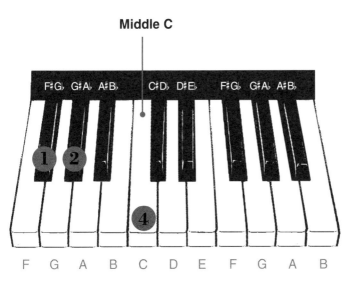

● use this note

1 2 3 4 or **5** use this finger

1 = thumb 2 = index finger 3 = middle finger 4 = ring finger 5 = little finger

Chord Spelling

1st (B♭), 3rd (D), #5th (F#), ♭7th (A♭), 9th (C)

B♭9-5
B♭ 9th Flattened 5th

Middle C

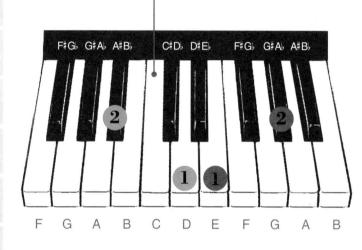

⬤ use this note

1 2 3 4 or **5** use this finger

1 = thumb 2 = index finger 3 = middle finger 4 = ring finger 5 = little finger

Chord Spelling

1st (B♭), 3rd (D), ♭5th (F♭), ♭7th (A♭), 9th (C)

Bb9/6
Bb 9th Add 6th

Middle C

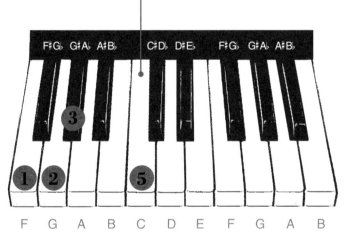

F♯G♭ G♯A♭ A♯B♭ C♯D♭ D♯E♭ F♯G♭ G♯A♭ A♯B♭

F G A B C D E F G A B

use this note

1 2 3 4 or **5** use this finger

1 = thumb   2 = index finger   3 = middle finger   4 = ring finger   5 = little finger

Chord Spelling

1st (Bb), 3rd (D), 5th (F), 6th (G), b7th (Ab), 9th (C)

B♭maj11
B♭ Major 11th

Middle C

use this note

1 2 3 4 or **5** use this finger

1 = thumb 2 = index finger 3 = middle finger 4 = ring finger 5 = little finger

Chord Spelling

1st (B♭), 3rd (D), 5th (F), 7th (A), 9th (C), 11th (E♭)

B♭m11
B♭ Minor 11th

Middle C

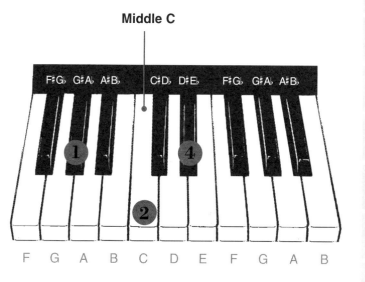

F G A B C D E F G A B

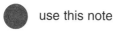 use this note

1 2 3 4 or 5 use this finger

1 = thumb 2 = index finger 3 = middle finger 4 = ring finger 5 = little finger

Chord Spelling

1st (B♭), ♭3rd (D♭), 5th (F), ♭7th (A♭), 9th (C), 11th (E♭)

Bb11
Bb Dominant 11th

Middle C

F#Gb G#Ab A#Bb   C#Db D#Eb   F#Gb G#Ab A#Bb

F   G   A   B   C   D   E   F   G   A   B

⬤ use this note

1 2 3 4 or **5** use this finger

1 = thumb   2 = index finger   3 = middle finger   4 = ring finger   5 = little finger

Chord Spelling

1st (Bb), 3rd (D), 5th (F), b7th (Ab), 9th (C), 11th (Eb)

B♭11-9
B♭ 11th Flattened 9th

Middle C

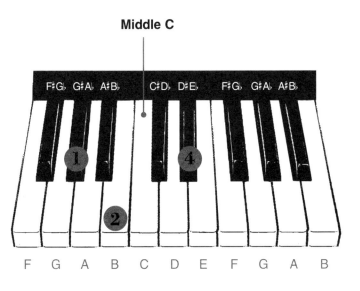

F G A B C D E F G A B

use this note

1 2 3 4 or **5** use this finger

1 = thumb   2 = index finger   3 = middle finger   4 = ring finger   5 = little finger

Chord Spelling

1st (B♭), 3rd (D), 5th (F), ♭7th (A♭), ♭9th (C♭), 11th (E♭)

4   **2**   **1**

B♭maj13
B♭ Major 13th

Middle C

F♯G♭ G♯A♭ A♯B♭ C♯D♭ D♯E♭ F♯G♭ G♯A♭ A♯B♭

3

1 **2** **5**

F G A B C D E F G A B

use this note

1 2 3 4 or **5** use this finger

1 = thumb   2 = index finger   3 = middle finger   4 = ring finger   5 = little finger

Chord Spelling

1st (B♭), 3rd (D), 5th (F), 7th (A), 9th (C), 11th (E♭), 13th (G)

B♭m13
B♭ Minor 13th

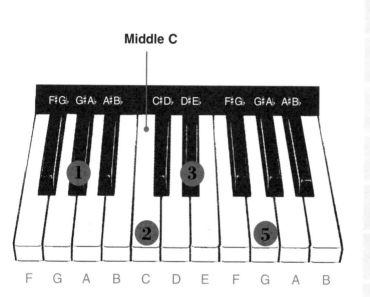

Middle C

use this note

1 2 3 4 or **5** use this finger

1 = thumb   2 = index finger   3 = middle finger   4 = ring finger   5 = little finger

Chord Spelling

(B♭), ♭3rd (D♭), 5th (F), ♭7th (A♭), 9th (C), 11th (E♭), 13th (G)

B♭13
B♭ Dominant 13th

Middle C

F♯G♭ G♯A♭ A♯B♭   C♯D♭ D♯E♭   F♯G♭ G♯A♭ A♯B♭

F G A B C D E F G A B

use this note

1 2 3 4 or **5** use this finger

1 = thumb 2 = index finger 3 = middle finger 4 = ring finger 5 = little finger

Chord Spelling

1st (B♭), 3rd (D), 5th (F), ♭7th (A♭), 9th (C), 11th (E♭), 13th (

B♭13-9
B♭ 13th Flattened 9th

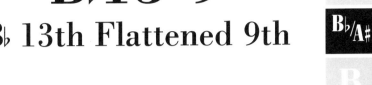

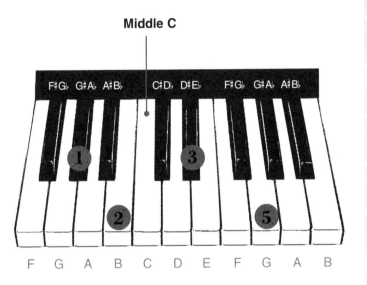

Middle C

use this note

1 2 3 4 or **5** use this finger

1 = thumb   2 = index finger   3 = middle finger   4 = ring finger   5 = little finger

Chord Spelling

t (B♭), 3rd (D), 5th (F), ♭7th (A♭), ♭9th (C♭), 11th (E♭), 13th (G)

B
B Major

Middle C

F G A B C D E F G A B

use this note

1 2 3 4 or **5** use this finger

1 = thumb 2 = index finger 3 = middle finger 4 = ring finger 5 = little finger

Chord Spelling

1st (B), 3rd (D#), 5th (F#)

Bm
B Minor

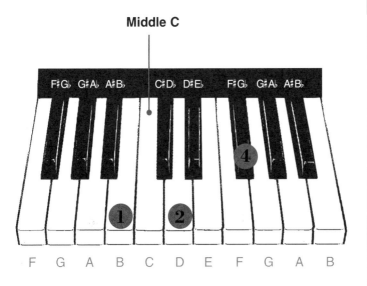

Middle C

use this note

1 2 3 4 or **5** use this finger

1 = thumb 2 = index finger 3 = middle finger 4 = ring finger 5 = little finger

Chord Spelling

1st (B), ♭3rd (D), 5th (F♯)

B+/Baug
B Augmented Triad

Middle C

F G A B C D E F G A B

 use this note

1 2 3 4 or **5** use this finger

1 = thumb   2 = index finger   3 = middle finger   4 = ring finger   5 = little finger

Chord Spelling

1st (B), 3rd (D#), #5th (Fx)

Bsus4
B Suspended 4th

Middle C

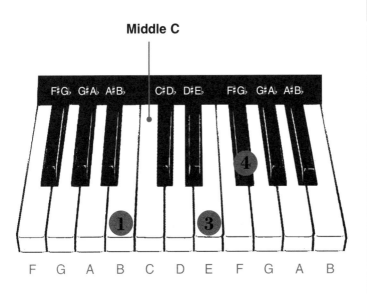

use this note

1 2 3 4 or **5**   use this finger

1 = thumb   2 = index finger   3 = middle finger   4 = ring finger   5 = little finger

Chord Spelling

1st (B), 4th (E), 5th (F♯)

Bo/Bdim
B Diminished Triad

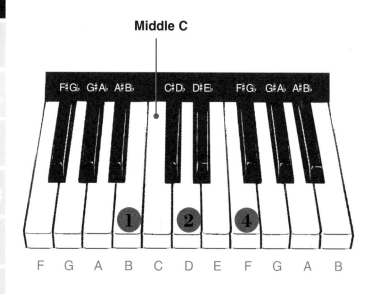

Middle C

use this note

1 2 3 4 or **5** use this finger

1 = thumb   2 = index finger   3 = middle finger   4 = ring finger   5 = little finger

Chord Spelling

1st (B), ♭3rd (D), ♭5th (F)

B6
B Major 6th

Middle C

F#G♭ G#A♭ A#B♭   C#D♭ D#E♭   F#G♭ G#A♭ A#B♭

F G A B C D E F G A B

● use this note

1 2 3 4 or **5** use this finger

1 = thumb   2 = index finger   3 = middle finger   4 = ring finger   5 = little finger

Chord Spelling

1st (B), 3rd (D#), 5th (F#), 6th (G#)

Bm6
B Minor 6th

Middle C

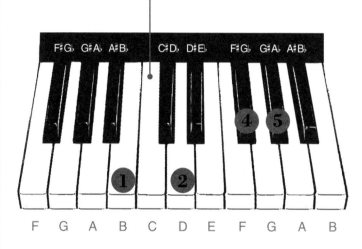

F G A B C D E F G A B

use this note

1 2 3 4 or **5** use this finger

1 = thumb   2 = index finger   3 = middle finger   4 = ring finger   5 = little finger

Chord Spelling

1st (B), ♭3rd (D), 5th (F#), 6th (G#)

Bmaj7
B Major 7th

Middle C

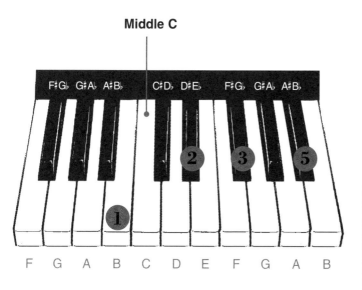

use this note

1 2 3 4 or **5** use this finger

1 = thumb   2 = index finger   3 = middle finger   4 = ring finger   5 = little finger

Chord Spelling

1st (B), 3rd (D#), 5th (F#), 7th (A#)

Bm7
B Minor 7th

Middle C

F♯G♭ G♯A♭ A♯B♭   C♯D♭ D♯E♭   F♯G♭ G♯A♭ A♯B♭

F G A B C D E F G A B

🔵 use this note

1 2 3 4 or **5** use this finger

1 = thumb   2 = index finger   3 = middle finger   4 = ring finger   5 = little finger

Chord Spelling

1st (B), ♭3rd (D), 5th (F♯), ♭7th (A)

B7
B Dominant 7th

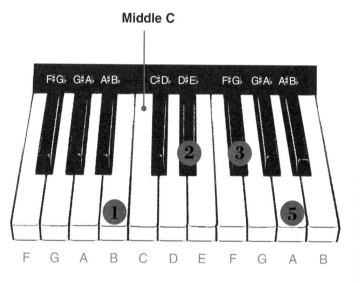

Middle C

F♯G♭ G♯A♭ A♯B♭   C♯D♭ D♯E♭   F♯G♭ G♯A♭ A♯B♭

F G A B C D E F G A B

use this note

1 2 3 4 or **5** use this finger

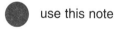

1 = thumb   2 = index finger   3 = middle finger   4 = ring finger   5 = little finger

Chord Spelling

1st (B), 3rd (D♯), 5th (F♯), ♭7th (A)

B7sus4
B Dominant 7th sus4

Middle C

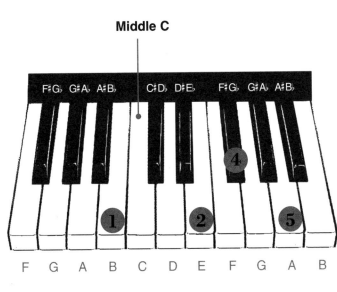

F#G♭ G#A♭ A#B♭   C#D♭ D#E♭   F#G♭ G#A♭ A#B♭

F G A B C D E F G A B

use this note

1 2 3 4 or **5** use this finger

1 = thumb   2 = index finger   3 = middle finger   4 = ring finger   5 = little finger

Chord Spelling

1st (B), 4th (E), 5th (F#), ♭7th (A)

B7+5
B Dominant 7th
Augmented 5th

Middle C

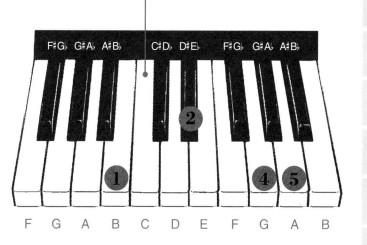

F G A B C D E F G A B

● use this note

1 2 3 4 or **5** use this finger

1 = thumb 2 = index finger 3 = middle finger 4 = ring finger 5 = little finger

Chord Spelling

1st (B), 3rd (D♯), ♯5th (Fx), ♭7th (A)

A
B♭/A♯
B
C
C♯/D♭
D
E♭/D♯
E
F
F♯/G♭
G
A♭/G♯

B7-5
B Dominant 7th
Flattened 5th

Middle C

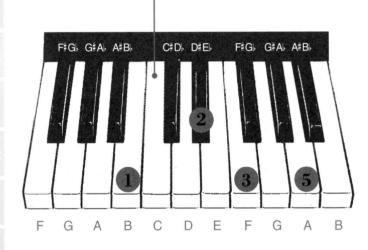

use this note

1 2 3 4 or **5** use this finger

1 = thumb   2 = index finger   3 = middle finger   4 = ring finger   5 = little finger

Chord Spelling

1st (B), 3rd (D#), ♭5th (F), ♭7th (A)

Bdim7
B Diminished 7th

B

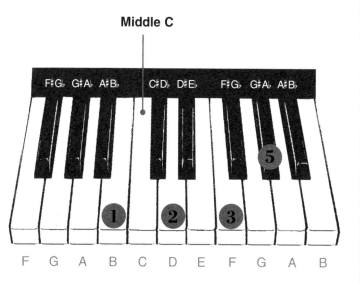

Middle C

F♯G♭ G♯A♭ A♯B♭   C♯D♭ D♯E♭   F♯G♭ G♯A♭ A♯B♭

F G A B C D E F G A B

● use this note

1 2 3 4 or **5** use this finger

1 = thumb 2 = index finger 3 = middle finger 4 = ring finger 5 = little finger

Chord Spelling

1st (B), ♭3rd (D), ♭5th (F), ♭♭7th (A♭)

Bm7-5
B Minor 7th
Flattened 5th

Middle C

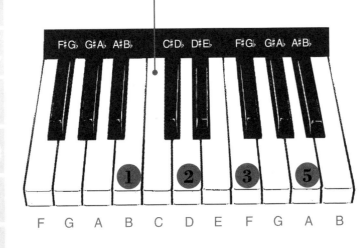

F G A B C D E F G A B

use this note

1 2 3 4 or **5** use this finger

1 = thumb 2 = index finger 3 = middle finger 4 = ring finger 5 = little finger

Chord Spelling

1st (B), ♭3rd (D), ♭5th (F), ♭7th (A)

Bmmaj7
B Minor-Major 7th

Middle C

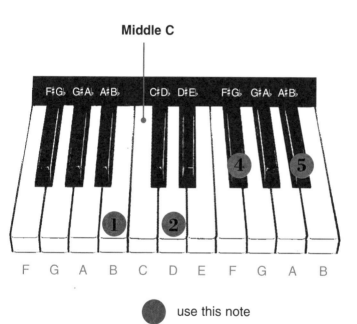

F G A B C D E F G A B

use this note

1 2 3 4 or **5** use this finger

1 = thumb   2 = index finger   3 = middle finger   4 = ring finger   5 = little finger

Chord Spelling

1st (B), ♭3rd (D), 5th (F♯), 7th (A♯)

Bmaj9
B Major 9th

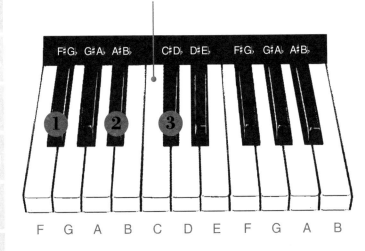

Middle C

F♯G♭ G♯A♭ A♯B♭   C♯D♭ D♯E♭   F♯G♭ G♯A♭ A♯B♭

F G A B C D E F G A B

use this note

1 2 3 4 or **5** use this finger

1 = thumb   2 = index finger   3 = middle finger   4 = ring finger   5 = little finger

Chord Spelling

1st (B), 3rd (D♯), 5th (F♯), 7th (A♯), 9th (C♯)

Bm9
B Minor 9th

Middle C

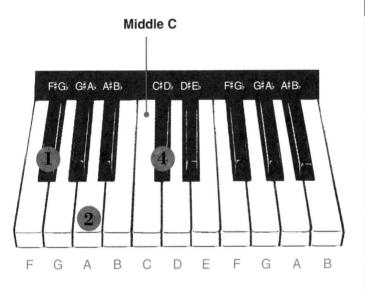

F G A B C D E F G A B

⬤ use this note

1 2 3 4 or **5** use this finger

1 = thumb   2 = index finger   3 = middle finger   4 = ring finger   5 = little finger

Chord Spelling

1st (B), ♭3rd (D), 5th (F♯), ♭7th (A), 9th (C♯)

B9
B Dominant 9th

Middle C

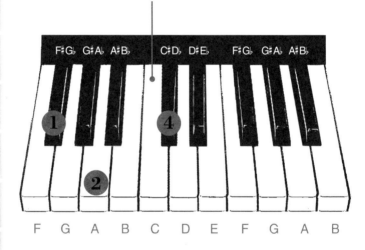

F G A B C D E F G A B

use this note

1 2 3 4 or **5** use this finger

1 = thumb 2 = index finger 3 = middle finger 4 = ring finger 5 = little finger

Chord Spelling

1st (B), 3rd (D#), 5th (F#), ♭7th (A), 9th (C#)

B9+5
B 9th Augmented 5th

Middle C

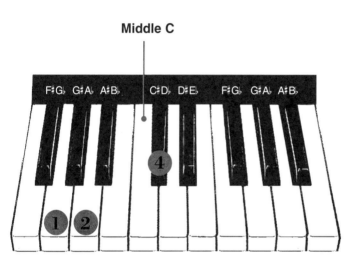

F G A B C D E F G A B

 use this note

1 2 3 4 or **5** use this finger

1 = thumb 2 = index finger 3 = middle finger 4 = ring finger 5 = little finger

Chord Spelling

1st (B), 3rd (D♯), ♯5th (Fx), ♭7th (A), 9th (C♯)

B9-5
B 9th Flattened 5th

Middle C

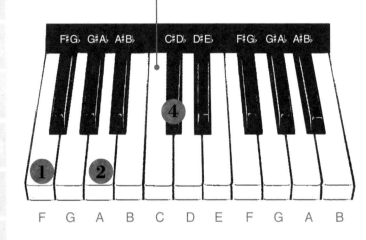

● use this note

1 2 3 4 or **5** use this finger

1 = thumb　2 = index finger　3 = middle finger　4 = ring finger　5 = little finger

Chord Spelling

1st (B), 3rd (D♯), ♭5th (F), ♭7th (A), 9th (C♯)

B9/6
B 9th Add 6th

Middle C

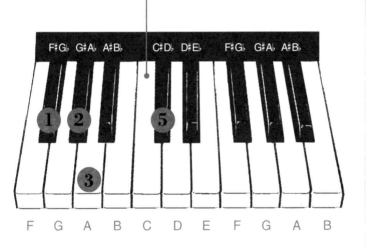

use this note

1 2 3 4 or **5** use this finger

1 = thumb   2 = index finger   3 = middle finger   4 = ring finger   5 = little finger

Chord Spelling

1st (B), 3rd (D#), 5th (F#), 6th (G#), ♭7th (A), 9th (C#)

Bmaj11
B Major 11th

Middle C

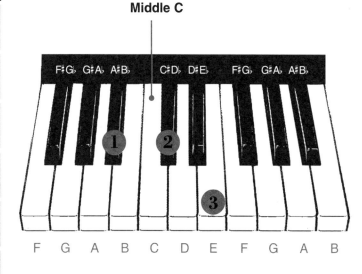

use this note

1 2 3 4 or **5** use this finger

1 = thumb   2 = index finger   3 = middle finger   4 = ring finger   5 = little finger

Chord Spelling

1st (B), 3rd (D#), 5th (F#), 7th (A#), 9th (C#), 11th (E)

Bm11
B Minor 11th

Middle C

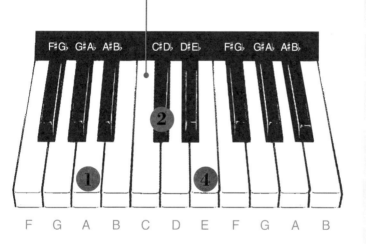

F#G♭ G#A♭ A#B♭   C#D♭ D#E♭   F#G♭ G#A♭ A#B♭

F G A B C D E F G A B

use this note

1 2 3 4 or **5**   use this finger

1 = thumb   2 = index finger   3 = middle finger   4 = ring finger   5 = little finger

Chord Spelling

1st (B), ♭3rd (D), 5th (F#), ♭7th (A), 9th (C#), 11th (E)

B11
B Dominant 11th

Middle C

use this note

1 2 3 4 or **5** use this finger

1 = thumb   2 = index finger   3 = middle finger   4 = ring finger   5 = little finger

Chord Spelling

1st (B), 3rd (D♯), 5th (F♯), ♭7th (A), 9th (C♯), 11th (E)

B11-9
B 11th Flattened 9th

Middle C

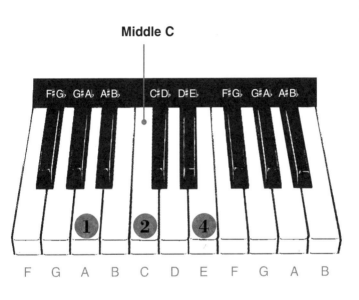

use this note

1 2 3 4 or **5** use this finger

1 = thumb   2 = index finger   3 = middle finger   4 = ring finger   5 = little finger

Chord Spelling

1st (B), 3rd (D#), 5th (F#), ♭7th (A), ♭9th (C), 11th (E)

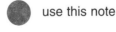

Bmaj13
B Major 13th

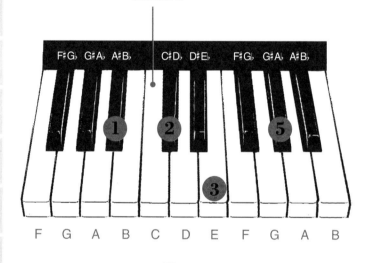

Middle C

F G A B C D E F G A B

use this note

1 2 3 4 or **5** use this finger

1 = thumb 2 = index finger 3 = middle finger 4 = ring finger 5 = little finger

Chord Spelling

1st (B), 3rd (D♯), 5th (F♯), 7th (A♯), 9th (C♯), 11th (E), 13th (C

Bm13
B Minor 13th

Middle C

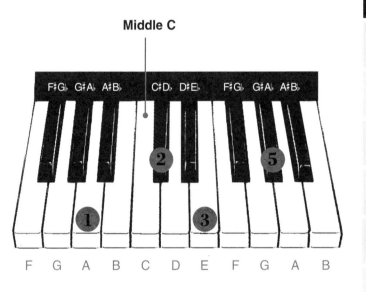

use this note

1 2 3 4 or **5** use this finger

1 = thumb 2 = index finger 3 = middle finger 4 = ring finger 5 = little finger

Chord Spelling

st (B), ♭3rd (D), 5th (F♯), ♭7th (A), 9th (C♯), 11th (E), 13th (G♯)

B13
B Dominant 13th

Middle C

use this note

1 2 3 4 or **5** use this finger

1 = thumb 2 = index finger 3 = middle finger 4 = ring finger 5 = little finger

Chord Spelling

1st (B), 3rd (D#), 5th (F#), ♭7th (A), 9th (C#), 11th (E), 13th (G)

B13-9
B 13th Flattened 9th

B

Middle C

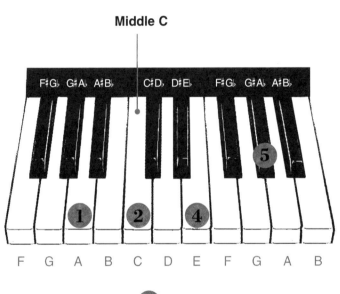

use this note

1 2 3 4 or **5** use this finger

1 = thumb   2 = index finger   3 = middle finger   4 = ring finger   5 = little finger

Chord Spelling

1st (B), 3rd (D#), 5th (F#), ♭7th (A), ♭9th (C), 11th (E), 13th (G#)

Inversions

Inversions are used to provide additional colouring to a harmony. They are chords which do not have their key (root) note as the bass (or bottom) note. For example, in its root (or normal) position, the chord of C major is made up of the key note (C) with the third (E) and fifth (G) notes above it.

The first inversion of C major would consist of E at the bottom with the notes G and C above it.

We have included the first inversions of the major, minor, dominant and diminished 7th chords that we showed earlier in the book. The first inversion chord can be used for any of the chords included in the book, following the example given above.

C
C Major
(1st inversion)

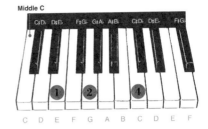

Chord Spelling
1st (E), 3rd (G), 5th (C)

C♯
C♯ Major
(1st inversion)

Chord Spelling
1st (E♯), 3rd (G♯), 5th (C♯)

D
D Major
(1st inversion)

Chord Spelling
1st (F♯), 3rd (A), 5th (D)

E♭
E♭ Major
(1st inversion)

Chord Spelling
1st (G), 3rd (B♭), 5th (E♭)

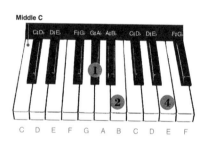

E
E Major
(1st inversion)

Chord Spelling
1st (G♯), 3rd (B), 5th (E)

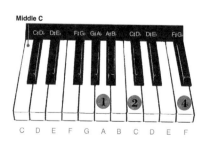

F
F Major
(1st inversion)

Chord Spelling
1st (A), 3rd (C), 5th (F)

F♯
F♯ Major
(1st inversion)

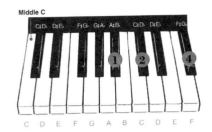

Chord Spelling
1st (A♯), 3rd (C♯), 5th (F♯)

G
G Major
(1st inversion)

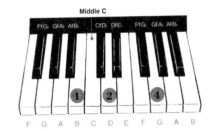

Chord Spelling
1st (B), 3rd (D), 5th (G)

A♭
A♭ Major
(1st inversion)

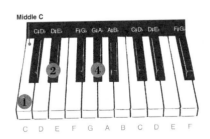

Chord Spelling
1st (C), 3rd (E♭), 5th (A♭)

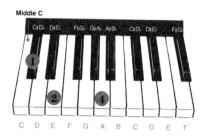

A
A Major
(1st inversion)

Chord Spelling
1st (C♯), 3rd (E), 5th (A)

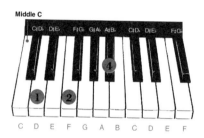

B♭
B♭ Major
(1st inversion)

Chord Spelling
1st (D), 3rd (F), 5th (B♭)

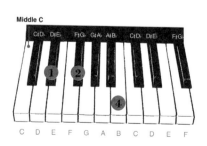

B
B Major
(1st inversion)

Chord Spelling
1st (D♯), 3rd (F♯), 5th (B)

Cm
C Minor
(1st inversion)

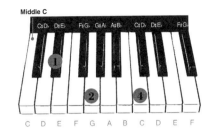

Chord Spelling
1st (E♭), 3rd (G), 5th (C)

C♯m
C♯ Minor
(1st inversion)

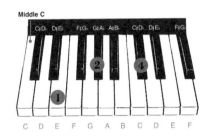

Chord Spelling
1st (E), 3rd (G♯), 5th (C♯)

Dm
D Minor
(1st inversion)

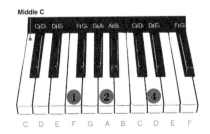

Chord Spelling
1st (F), 3rd (A), 5th (D)

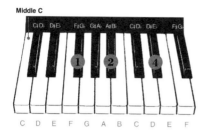

E♭m
E♭ Minor
(1st inversion)

Chord Spelling
1st (G♭), 3rd (B♭), 5th (E♭)

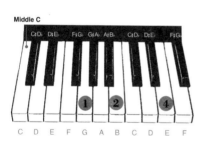

Em
E Minor
(1st inversion)

Chord Spelling
1st (G), 3rd (B), 5th (E)

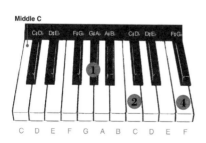

Fm
F Minor
(1st inversion)

Chord Spelling
1st (A♭), 3rd (C), 5th (F)

F♯m
F♯ Minor
(1st inversion)

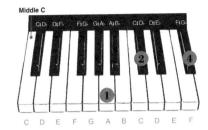

Chord Spelling
1st (A), 3rd (C♯), 5th (F♯)

Gm
G Minor
(1st inversion)

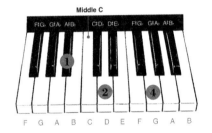

Chord Spelling
1st (B♭), 3rd (D), 5th (G)

A♭m
A♭ Minor
(1st inversion)

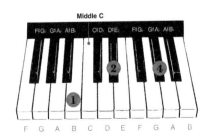

Chord Spelling
1st (C♭), 3rd (E♭), 5th (A♭)

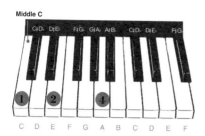

Am
A Minor
(1st inversion)

Chord Spelling
1st (C), 3rd (E), 5th (A)

B♭m
B♭ Minor
(1st inversion)

Chord Spelling
1st (D♭), 3rd (F), 5th (B♭)

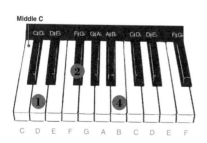

Bm
B Minor
(1st inversion)

Chord Spelling
1st (D), 3rd (F♯), 5th (B)

C7
C Dominant 7th
(1st inversion)

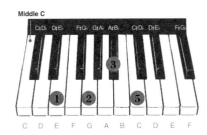

Chord Spelling
1st (E), 3rd (G), 5th (B♭),
7th (C)

C#7
C# Dominant 7th
(1st inversion)

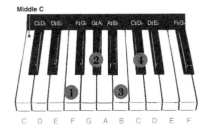

Chord Spelling
1st (E#), 3rd (G#), 5th (B),
7th (C#)

D7
D Dominant 7th
(1st inversion)

Chord Spelling
1st (F#), 3rd (A), 5th (C),
7th (D)

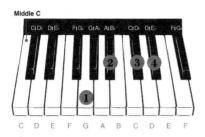

E♭7
E♭ Dominant 7th
(1st inversion)

Chord Spelling
1st (G), 3rd (B♭), 5th (D♭),
7th (E♭)

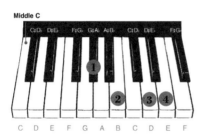

E7
E Dominant 7th
(1st inversion)

Chord Spelling
1st (G♯), 3rd (B), 5th (D),
7th (E)

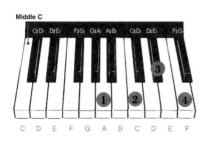

F7
F Dominant 7th
(1st inversion)

Chord Spelling
1st (A), 3rd (C), 5th (E♭),
7th (F)